GOOD HOUSEKEEPING

Household
HINTS

GOOD HOUSEKEEPING

Household
HINTS

The essential home facts

BCA

LONDON NEW YORK SYDNEY TORONTO

This edition published 1993
by BCA
by arrangement with Ebury Press
Random House
20 Vauxhall Bridge Road
London SW1V 2SA

CN 1642

British Library Cataloguing in Publication Data
Budge, Erica
  Household hints
  1. Housework, – Manuals
I. Title II. Series
648

The Good Housekeeping Institute is the food and consumer research
centre of *Good Housekeeping* magazine.

Consultant
GILLIAN SMEDLEY, *Director of Communications of the Good
Housekeeping Institute*
Text by
Erica Budge
Edited by
Sarah Bailey

The information contained in this book was checked as rigorously as
possible before going to press. The publisher accepts no responsibility
for any changes which may have occurred since, nor for any other
variance of fact from that recorded here in good faith.

Typeset by Textype Typesetting, Cambridge
Printed and bound in Great Britain by
Mackays of Chatham PLC, Chatham, Kent

Contents

Addresses

This general list is intended as a starting point for your enquiries. For emergencies, power or supply failure or information about appliances for electricity, gas and water, check in your local telephone directory. It will also have the number of your local CORGI (Confederation for the Registration of Gas Installers) Office. It is a good idea to make a list of emergency phone numbers for gas electricity and water, and keep it near the telephone (together with your plumber's number) for quick, easy reference.

The Electricity Council 30 Millbank London SW1   01 834 2333

The Electricity Consumers Council Brook House Torrington Place London WC1   01 636 5703

BEAB *(British Electrotechnical Approvals Board)* Mark House Queen's Road Hersham Walton on Thames KT12 5NA   0932 244401

British Gas plc Rivermill House 152 Grosvenor Road London SW1   01 821 1444

Gas Consumer Council Abford House 15 Wilton Road London SW1   01 931 9155

Water Authorities Association 1 Queen's Anne's Gate London SW1   01 222 0106

Institute of Plumbing 64 Station Lane Hornchurch Essex   04024 77791

Solid Fuel Advisory Service Hobart House Grosvenor Place London SW1X 7AE   01 235 2020

Consumers Association 14 Buckingham Street London WC2N 6DS   01 839 1222

The British Standards Institute 2 Park Street London W1   01 629 9000

The Design Centre 28 Haymarket London SW1   01 839 8000

The Building Centre 26 Store Street London WC1   0344 884999   *(this is a Winkfield Row number which deals with general enquiries and will pass you on to the relevant department.)*

Association of British Laundry, Cleaning and Rental Services Ltd 7 Churchill Court 58 Station Road North Harrow Middlesex HA2 7SA   01 863 7755   *(Call 01 863 8658 for The Drycleaning Information Bureau and 01 863 9178 for The Laundry Information Service.)*

British Toy and Hobby Manufacturers Association 80 Camberwell Road London SE5   01 7091 7271

Glass and Glazing Federation 44–48 Borough High Street London SE1 1XB   01 403 7177

Scotchgard Treatment *Applied by Scotchgard licensed applicators. For your nearest dealer, dial 100 and ask for Freephone 1002*

VEDC *(Vitreous Enamel Development Council)* New House High Street Ticehurst Wadhurst Sussex TN5 7AL   0580 200152

RoSPA *(Royal Society for the Prevention of Accidents)* Cannon House The Priory Queensway Birmingham B4 6BS   0212 002461   *(The London Office is staffed for only part of the week but can be reached on 01 235 6889. The address is 1 Grosvenor Crescent London SW1.)*

British Red Cross National Headquarters 9 Grosvenor Crescent London SW1   01 235 5454

RSPCA The Causeway Horsham Sussex   0403 64181

Institute of Horticulture 80 Vincent Square London SW1   01 834 4333

1

Safety first

Safety in the home should be your priority at all times, even when carrying out the most mundane tasks. Here are some thought-provoking statistics:

- There are over 2 million accidents in the home a year which require hospital treatment.

- 4,500 of these accidents are fatal.

- The kitchen can be a dangerous place: 58,000 falls and 100,000 cuts happen in kitchens every year

Do not let familiarity breed contempt. With a little fore-thought and some preventative action you can avoid major accidents in your home.

Below are some general tips to help you keep your home as safe as possible. The *Emergency Action* section on page 138 offers advice if an accident does occur.

SAFETY RULES FOR THE HOME

- Store sharp knives out of the way in a drawer or knife rack.

- Mop up spills immediately, and keep the floor clean.

- Discourage clutter.

- Keep things you need daily within easy reach.

- Do not stand on chairs to reach top shelves. Invest in a step stool or a pair of steps with a top handle for steadying yourself.

- Secure loose rugs and carpets.

- Make sure that stairs are adequately lit.

- If your household includes children, elderly people or pets (or all three), make sure that all fire guards are fixed securely to the wall.

- Fit a coiled lead to electric kettles, to avoid trailing flex.

- When cooking, turn all panhandles to the side of the hob and make sure gas kettle spouts turn towards the wall. Not only children can accidentally pull saucepans off the stove.

- If you have children, fit a hob guard on the stove.

- Wear gloves, goggles and/or masks if instructed to do so when working on DIY jobs.

- If you are using any potentially dangerous materials or tools in the same room as a small child, always take the child with you if you have to answer the door or phone.

- Switch off and unplug appliances when not in use, and overnight.

- Do not take hairdryers or other electrical appliances into bathrooms.

Household chemicals

- If you have to use aerosol products, use ones which are free from chlorofluorocarbons (CFCs) and should not damage the ozone layer.

- Household bleach and disinfectant are the two commonest causes of poisoning among household chemicals. Keep them away from children.

- There is no logic in storing household bleach and cleaning agents under the sink. If possible store them on shelves or in cupboards at eye-level for you and out of reach of children. In this position they are easy for you to reach without bending down and fumbling in cupboards.

- Always follow the manufacturers' instructions on proprietary adhesives, aerosols, etc. (Before you buy, read the instructions carefully to ensure that you do actually need what you are buying.)

- Never use solvents, paints or adhesives in the same room as naked flames. Extinguish pilot lights in the kitchen if that is where you are working.

- Never mix lavatory cleaner with any other kind of cleaning materials in the lavatory bowl; this can cause toxic fumes.

- Never decant chemicals into other containers, especially soft drinks bottles. (Some chemicals can dissolve plastics.)

Poisons and medicines

- Keep all medicines out of reach of children, in a lockable cupboard in the kitchen (very few people need medicine in the bathroom) so you can keep an eye on them.

- If you or a member of the family do need medication regularly at night or in the morning, keep your supplies in a lockable cabinet in the bathroom or bedroom, whichever is more convenient.

- Dispose of unused prescribed medicine immediately. Take it back to the chemist if you are not sure what to do.

- Lock away all solvents, glue and stain removal kits when they are not in use.

- Store small jars/packets of poisonous substances still in their packaging in screw top jars. Label the jars as well.

- Do not bulk-buy proprietary medicines or poisonous substances. Buy what you need at the time, so you are not left with surplus (and possibly dangerous) substances.

Fire practice

- Last thing at night, check that all internal doors are closed. A wooden door can hold back the spread of fire.

- Switch off and unplug all electrical appliances not in use.

- Check that all ashtrays have been emptied.

- Bank down all solid fuel open fires before you go to bed. It may not be possible to extinguish them completely. In all cases, keep a fireguard securely fixed at the fireplace.

- Have chimneys swept regularly.

- Have a fire escape plan and make sure all the household know what it is. Have fire practices regularly.

- If you fit smoke detectors, look for BS No. 5446 part 1 and the BS Kitemark. Remember to change the batteries once a year.

- Don't store newspapers, rags and cleaning fluids under the stairs. If they caught fire, they would cut off your escape route.

- Never use aerosols near naked flames or leave spray cans near a heat source (sunshine, heaters, lamps). They could explode.

- Remember that it is illegal to leave a child under the age of 12 (7 in Scotland) alone in a room with an unguarded heater or fire.

Chip pan/deep fryer

Accidents with a chip pan are a major cause of fires in the home.

- NEVER leave a deep fryer unattended.

- Keep a wrung out tea towel to hand whenever you use the fryer, to throw over it if there is a flare up.

- Do not fill the pan more than ⅓ full.

- Do not put in wet chips (dry them in kitchen paper first).

- Do not exceed given temperatures.

- If the pan does catch fire, try to turn off the heat source. Throw the cloth over the pan, or cover flames with a lid or a metal baking tray.

  DO NOT THROW WATER ON A CHIP PAN FIRE.

- Never try to move the fryer while it is still hot.

- If you cannot control the fire, get everyone out of the house, shut the kitchen door and call the fire brigade.

2

Material facts

It is a well known fact that clothes and textiles last longer if they are cleaned and laundered correctly, mended as soon as any tears and holes appear and stored properly when not in use. The following tips are designed to help you do this.

Laundering at the correct temperature with the correct detergent is the best preserver of clothes and household linens. Always read the fabric care instructions on the care label carefully and act upon them. The laundry code was revised in 1986, and the charts provided on pages 18-21 will be useful as most people will have some pre-1986 clothes with old care labelling. The charts show both old and new symbols for washing, tumble drying, ironing and dry cleaning.

Hard and soft water

How well detergent and soap perform depends very much on the hardness of your water supply.

Hard water contains calcium and magnesium salts which reduce the efficiency of soap, leaving unsightly grey scum in sinks and baths and limescale on the heating element and other important metal parts of washing machines, dishwashers and kettles which will make them more expensive to run.

Call your local water board to find out the degree of hardness in your water. If it is hard, here are some remedies:

- Use Calgon water softener in the washing machine. This will make your washing powder more efficient and protect the machine parts from lingering death by limescale.

- Use a slow-release water softener cartridge (eg Micromet) in the cold water storage tank. This is simply suspended in the water tank; it lasts about 6 months, and replacement cartridges are available.

GENERAL TIPS

Washing machines

- Look after your machine. Wipe off condensation following use. Polish casing occasionally with a wax-free spray polish.

- Run through your standard wash cycle with clear water every three months or so to clean out the machine.

- Wash out the powder dispenser drawer regularly. Scrub out the small holes in the fabric conditioner section of the drawer with an old toothbrush.

- Check the rubber seal of the door regularly. (These are inexpensive to replace.)

- Do up all zips and buttons and empty pockets before loading clothes into washing machines. Small coins and toys can get through the drum and block the pump.

- Read the instructions and advice in the washing machine manufacturer's booklet. Most give you a list of checkpoints to run through if the machine does not function.

- Keep washing machine (and tumble dryer) instruction booklets in a clearview plastic wallet *near the washing machine*.

Tumble dryers

- Check that buttons and zips are fastened and that there are no pens, coins etc. in the pockets. Hard or metal objects can chip the enamel off the inner drum of the dryer.

- Articles will dry more quickly if the dryer is only half-full.

- Clean out the tumble dryer filter after each cycle. Most tumble dryers now have them fitted in the door.

- Make sure that your tumble dryer can ventilate properly. Follow the manufacturer's instructions in the leaflet accompanying the machine.

- Clean out the warm air vent at the back of the machine regularly. Use an old baby bottle brush or soft toothbrush, slightly dampened to pick up recalcitrant fluff.

- When choosing a dryer, consider the advantages of a time delay switch which will allow you to programme the machine to switch on at night when electricity is cheaper. (One full load averages 2½ kilowatt hours, or 2½ units on the meter.)

Irons

- Keep your iron clean. Use a proprietary iron cleaner stick, to keep the bottom clean and smooth running. (Irons with non-stick coating on the base plate are now available. Consider one of these if you are replacing your iron.)

- Clean starch marks from an iron by rubbing it while still warm with a cake of soap. Polish off with a clean cloth.

- Empty steam irons after each use, or the vents may become blocked by furring. Use a proprietary descaler regularly.

- Check the iron flex regularly, and replace immediately if it is frayed.

- Choose an ironing board that can be adjusted to your height, to avoid backache.

- Replace your ironing board cover as soon as it shows sign of wear.

- Avoid ironing boards with asbestos pad iron rests. (These should only appear on old models.)

Dry-cleaning

- Be careful when using coin-op dry-cleaning machines. They provide a general cleaning service which may not suit your garment. Check with the care label on the article to be cleaned. If in doubt, it is best to go to a professional dry-cleaners.

- Never use coin-op dry-cleaning machines for duvets or other bedding. Lingering fumes from the dry-cleaning solvent could prove fatal.

- Always hang dry-cleaned clothes and curtains or upholstery covers out to air before using. Dry cleaning fumes are toxic and can cling in the folds of heavy material. Do not hang clothes in an enclosed wardrobe for a day or so.

- When driving home with dry-cleaned articles in the car, keep the window open.

Revised textile care labelling code

Old Symbol	New Symbol	Accompanying Wording	Washing temperature	
			Machine	Hand
[1 95°]	[95]	'wash in cotton cycle/ programme' or 'wash as cotton'	very hot 95°C *normal action, rinse and spin*	hand hot 50°C
[2 60°]	[60]	'wash in cotton cycle/ programme' or 'wash as cotton'	hot 60°C *normal action, rinse and spin*	hand hot 50°C
[4 50°]	[50 —]	'wash in synthetics cycle/ programme' or 'wash as synthetics'	hand hot 50°C *reduced action, cold rinse,* *reduced spin or drip dry*	
[5 40°]	[40]	'wash in cotton cycle/ programme' or 'wash as cotton'	warm 40°C *normal action, rinse and spin*	
[6 40°]	[40 —]	'wash in synthetics cycle/ programme' or 'wash as synthetics'	warm 40°C *reduced action, cold rinse,* *reduced spin*	
[7 40°]	[40 ==]	'wash in wool cycle/ programme' or 'wash as wool'	warm 40°C *much reduced action,* *normal rinse and spin*	
[hand]	[hand]	Hand wash	See garment label	
[✗]	[✗]	Do not wash		

Washing Temperatures

100°C   Boil   Self explanatory

95°C   Very hot   Water heated to near boiling temperature.

60°C   Hot   Hotter than the hand can bear. The temperature of water coming from many domestic hot taps.

50°C   Hand hot   As hot as the hands can bear.

40°C   Warm   Pleasantly warm to the hand.

18

Fabric type

Used for white cotton and linen articles without special finishes, this process provides the most vigorous wash conditions. The high water temperature and maximum agitation and spinning times ensure good whiteness and stain removal.

For cotton, linen or viscose articles without special finishes where colours are fast at 60°C. Provides vigorous wash conditions but at a temperature which maintains fast colours.

For nylon; polyester/cotton mixtures; polyester; cotton and viscose articles with special finishes; cotton/acrylic mixtures. Reduced agitation and the lower wash temperature safeguards the finish and colour. Cold rinsing followed by short spinning minimises creases.

Suited to cotton, linen and viscose articles where colours are fast at 40°C but not at 60°C. This process ensures thorough cleansing but at the lower wash temperature essential to safeguard colour fastness

For those articles which require gentle, low temperature laundering to preserve colour and shape and minimise creasing eg acrylics; acetate and triacetate, including mixtures with wool; polyester/wool blends.

For wool, including blankets, wool mixed with other fibres, and silk, requiring low temperature washing with minimum agitation. This treatment preserves colour, size and handle. Do not rub or hand wring.

Include articles with Programme 3 60°C care label in 50

Include articles with Programme 8 30°C care label in 40 or 40

Significance of the Bar underneath the Wash Tub

Absence of bar denotes normal (maximum) machine action and is labelled 'wash as cotton'

A bar denotes reduced (medium) machine action and is labelled 'wash as synthetics'.

A broken bar denotes much reduced (minimum) wash action and labelled 'wash as wool'.

Mixing Wash Loads
You can mix wash labels without a bar provided you wash at the lowest temperature shown.

You can mix wash labels with and without a bar provided that you wash at the lowest temperature, BUT you must reduce the wash action.

Articles with 40 must be washed as wool at a much reduced wash action.

'Wash separately' means what it says.

Bleaching

This symbol indicates that household (chlorine) bleach could be used. Care must be taken to follow the manufacturer's instructions.

When this symbol appears on a label household bleach must *not* be used.

Ironing

The number of dots in the ironing symbol indicates the correct temperature setting – the fewer the dots the cooler the iron setting.

| cool | warm | hot | do not iron |

Dry Cleaning

The letter in the circle refers to the solvent which may be used in the dry-cleaning process, and those using 'coin op' dry-cleaning should check that the cleaning symbol shown on the label is the same as that in the instructions given on the front of the machine.

Goods normal for dry-cleaning in all solvents.

Goods normal for dry-cleaning in perchloroethylene, white spirit, Solvent 113 and Solvent 11.

Goods normal for dry-cleaning in white spirit or Solvent 113.

Do not dry-clean.

N.B. When the circle containing P or F is underlined, do not 'coin op' clean, as this indicates that these materials are sensitive to dry cleaning and require special treatment.

Drying

Care labels may also include one or other of the following symbols recommending a particular drying method.

Tumble dry on a low heat setting.

Tumble dry on a high heat setting.

Do not tumble dry.

Where the prohibition symbol above is used, further instructions, such as 'dry flat' for heavy knitted garments, should be given in words.

IDENTIFYING MAN-MADE FIBRES

Fibre Brand Names	Man-made Fibre Group	Fibre-Brand Names	Man-Made Fibre Group
Dicel	ACETATE	Dacron	
		Diolen	
Acrilan		Fortrel	
Courtelle		Mitrelle	
Dolan	ACRYLIC	Quallofil	
Dralon		Tergal	POLYESTER
Orlon		Terinda	
		Terlenka	
Lycra	ELASTANE	Terylene	
		Trevira	
Lurex	METALLIC		
Acrilan SEF	MODACRYLIC	Meraklon	POLYPROPYLENE
Kanekalon	(Flame retard-		
Teklan	ant properties)	Arnel	TRIACETATE
		Tricel	
Antron			
Bri-nylon		Danufil	
Cantrece		Danuflor	
Enka Nylon		Durafil	
Enka Perlon		Evlan	VISCOSE
Qazul	NYLON	Fibro	
Quintesse	(POLYAMIDE)	Sarille	
Tactel		Viloft	
Tactesse			
Tendrelle			
Timbrelle			

Note: Some items of clothing and household textiles/articles may carry a fibre content label indicating the fibre group, eg acetate, nylon, instead of the brand name of the fibre.

CLOTHES

Stains

- Deal with all stains immediately if possible.

- Keep a stain removing kit handy. A good selection includes methylated spirit, lighter fuel, amyl acetate, white spirit, ammonia, hydrogen peroxide, nail varnish remover and glycerine. They must be kept only in small quantities, in well-stoppered, clearly labelled bottles. All of these substances are poisonous, and must be locked away whenever you are not using them.

- You will probably keep some of these substances for other purposes (eg methylated spirit, turpentine, nail varnish remover). Nevertheless, it is a good idea to keep duplicate small bottles in your stain removal kit. When you need them in a hurry, you will not have to rummage in tool cupboards or dressing tables.

- Proprietary stain removers can be bought, and can be useful if you have recurrent similar stains – felt tip pens, for example. These stain removers must also be safely locked away. Stain Devils is a well-known brand. When using any stain-removing solvent, follow these rules:

  — Always wear rubber gloves.

  — Never smoke.

  — Never work in a room with open fires or radiant heaters.

  — Turn off pilot lights.

  — Leave the window open, or at least open a door.

- Keep calm when tackling stains. Scrape or blot off as much as possible first, then test the stain remover on an unobtrusive part of the garment.

- Always treat a ring round the stain first, then work from the outside inwards to prevent spreading. Dab on solvent with a pad of white absorbent cotton cloth. Dye from a coloured applicator could be loosened by certain solvents, causing additional staining.

For more information on stain removal, see GH practical library *How to Remove Stains*.

Washing

- Brush mud and dirt from clothes as soon as it is dry. There is no point in putting muddy clothes in the washing machine.

- Remove stains you know will not be cleaned by laundering before washing. They could become 'set' by the laundering process.

- Always use the correct amount of detergent. If you underdose, in the name of economy, you will not be supplying enough soil-suspending agent. Dirt will migrate back into your clothes during the wash cycle.

- If you overdose on low-lathering powder, nothing will happen (other than a waste of money). However overdosing with high-lather powder will produce too much foam, which will then crowd the clothes, prevent effective washing and may even cause overflow.

- Always use low-lather detergent in front-loading washing machines. Too much foam will cause seepage through the door.

- Always use the correct amount of fabric conditioner. If you use too much, your clothes will become greasy to the touch and will eventually fail to absorb detergent solution and so stay dirty even though they are washed as recommended. A build-up of fabric conditioner on towels will reduce their absorbency.

- Sort your washing into matching loads according to the information on the care label (see page 18).

- Keep your washing powder packet in a strong plastic bag to protect it from wet hands and surfaces.

- Always wash full loads if possible. (Some washing machines have a half-load capacity.) It is more economic.

- Do not use half-load facility for a small load of synthetics; they need a full load of water to prevent creasing.

- You can wash mixed loads of fabrics if it is not possible to make a full load of the same sort of washing. Set the washing machine programme to suit the lowest temperature indicated on the care labels. This can mean some part of the load will be underwashed. Make sure that these articles are laundered at their correct temperature every three washes at least.

- Never mix white and strong-coloured fabric.

- Always mend tears and holes before washing, as the washing action will make them larger.

- Close all zips, Velcro and buttoned openings before washing. If left open, they may snag other garments.

- Check all pockets for pens, money, paper handkerchiefs etc. Pens will leak during the wash cycle and paper tissues disintegrate into far more pieces than you would have thought possible.

- Tie up all loose tapes, apron strings etc, otherwise they may get torn off.

- Wash tiny articles tied up in an old pillowcase. This prevents them from getting lost or entangled in larger garments.

- Test for colour fastness before washing suspect fabric. Dampen a seam allowance, and place it between two white handkerchiefs. Press with your iron set at the temperature suitable for the fabric on test. If the colour runs into the white handkerchiefs, wash the article separately.

- Do not soak white nylon fabric with coloured fabrics as nylon is quick to pick up loose dye and floating grime.

- If the instructions on your garment tell you to wash separately for the first few times, do just that. To test for colour fastness after the first few washes, add an old white handkerchief to the wash. If the handkerchief remains white, the garment may be washed with other articles.

Hand washing

- Dissolve washing powder properly first in a little hot water. Add this to the hand-hot water you use for the wash.

- Dissolve washing powder completely before adding garments, otherwise you may get colour spotting.

- When soaking, immerse the whole article in case there is a slight colour change.

- Rinse hand-washed synthetics in cold water before drying; this helps prevent creases.

Wool

- Before washing a woollen garment, trace its outline onto a stout piece of card. Then you can stretch it back to its correct size and shape after washing.

- Do up buttons, zips or fasteners before washing.

- Squeeze the soapy water through the garment, never rub the wool.

- Add 5 ml/1 tsp glycerine to washing and rinsing water to help keep wool soft. (Light duty washing products, intended for woollens, will also leave fibres soft.)

- After rinsing, squeeze gently without wringing, then roll the article in a towel to press out remaining water.

- Make sure buttons, zips or fasteners are still closed, pull garment into shape and allow to dry flat on an old towel. Keep away from direct heat and/or bright sunshine.

- Push empty tubes from kitchen paper or foil into the sleeves while the garment dries flat.

Silk

- Wash silk as wool, rolling in a towel to dry. Iron on the wrong side when still damp, unless it is wild or tussore silk, which should be ironed when completely dry.

Drying

- Do not leave damp clothes hanging over varnished or polished wood. It could cause staining and also mark the wood.

- Never leave damp coloured and damp white fabrics in the same basket. The dyes could transfer.

- Dry deep-dyed articles flat until the dye is fixed. If line-dried at this stage, dye may trickle down leaving unsightly patches.

- Dry synthetic sweaters on the line with the help of old tights. Thread a leg through each armhole and pull the middle of the tights through the neckhole. Peg the tights on the line, not the sweater. Then you will avoid peg marks and stretching.

Tumble drying

- Do not tumble dry garments to bone dryness. They will be too creased to iron.

- Do not tumble dry light coloured towels with dark items as the fluff may be transferred.

Ironing

- Don't iron everything in an excess of virtue. Modern synthetics often look better if they are hung up on hangers straight from the tumble dryer.

- When using a steam iron, wait until it reaches the desired temperature, otherwise it may drip onto your clothes.

- Always match temperatures on the iron and care labels correctly. The thermostats on modern irons are very sensitive.

- When ironing a garment with decorative stitching, press on a towel and the wrong side only to raise the stitches.

- Leave pleats until last when ironing. Tackle each pleat separately, or two at a time if they are small. Use the pressing cloth folded double as pleats need more moisture.

- If a garment is heavy and therefore pulls the pleats apart during ironing, place a chair under the ironing board for the surplus to rest on.

- When pressing hems, iron on the garment edge only, otherwise the stitch marks of the hem itself will be imprinted on the outside of the garment.

- If clothes have become too dry for ironing, put them in a plastic bag and sprinkle with water. Close the bag and leave for a few hours (but not more than 24).

- Small amounts of dried out washing can be made ironable by putting them in the fridge for 5 or 10 minutes.

- Try to iron ahead; freshly ironed clothes worn immediately crease more quickly than clothes allowed to hang for a while.

- Iron starched items on the right side. It keeps them clean for longer.

- If you need a sleeveboard, improvise by wrapping a rolling pin in a thick towel.

- Iron velvet on the wrong side on 2 or 3 layers of towel so that the pile does not become crushed.

- When using spray starch or retexturiser at the ironing board, put newspapers on the floor first. Drifting spray can make the floor dangerously slippery.

- There is a correct way to iron clothes (see panel). Set the iron to the lowest recommended temperature (slightly hotter if you are using a damp pressing cloth). Press on the wrong side (WS) first, then the right side (RS). Move the garment away from you as you go, so that you do not lean on ironed sections.

The Ironing Sequence

Shirt/Blouse	Skirt	Trousers
Sleeve opening edge	(Inside out)	Fly extension
Cuff (inside first)	Lining	Zipper and below
Sleeve	Waistband	waistband
Shoulder	(Right side)	Waistband
Button band (WS)	Waistband	Inside leg
Button band (RS)	Body of skirt	Outside leg
Body	(start at lower	(do one leg at a
Collar (underside	end)	time)
first)		

Questions and Answers

Q. *My black clothes always fade into grey after a few washes. What can I do about it?*

A. The faded look is usually the result of washing powder build-up. Soak the clothes in a bowl of warm water to which you have added half a cup of vinegar.

Q. *I have mistakenly washed a mixed load and the colours have run. How can I retrieve the situation?*

A. Read the garment labels first. If they are suitable (ie fast coloured and washable), soak them in a solution of Stain Devils Stainsalts, or Dylon's Run Away colour run remover. Rinse; launder at the highest temperature appropriate to the fabric. (Do not use on garments with a non colourfast pattern or trim.)

Q. *I have a deep-dyed cotton dress which has faded in patches and lost colour overall. What can be done to revive it?*

A. You can remove all the dye with Dylon's Pre-dye. This strips all the colour from garments made of 100 per cent cotton. Then you can re-dye it.

Q. *How can I prevent corduroy trousers from fading and looking grey after washing?*

A. Turn them inside out. This cuts down friction during laundering which could flatten the pile and make it appear faded. You can help to prevent denim from fading by turning jeans inside out, but as faded jeans are *de rigeur* you may not be thanked for it.

CLOTHES MAINTENANCE

Alterations

- Do not undo old stitching until you have marked or sewn the new line.

- Old stitch marks can be a useful guide, so do not press out until you have finished the alteration.

- Where practicable, stick to the golden rule: sew first, cut afterwards.

- Don't overdo it. If you want to alter a garment, do not cut it to pieces all at once. Do it a piece at a time.

- Mark new lines on the wrong side (WS) with tailor's chalk.

- Always have your iron set up when dressmaking or altering. Keep an empty roll-on deodorant bottle filled with water. This makes an excellent device to damp seam allowances before ironing. (It can also be used for stubborn creases in the body of a garment.)

- In an emergency, you can fix up a dangling hem using double-sided adhesive tape.

Briefs/knickers

- To avoid the recurrence of Thrush infection, you can sterilize your knickers in the microwave. Lay freshly-washed knickers on kitchen towels and place in the oven. Turn it on to high and leave for five minutes. DO NOT LEAVE MICROWAVE UNATTENDED DURING THIS OPERATION.

Buttons

- Cut off and save the buttons from good quality garments. They can dress up sale bargains.

- Don't sew buttons on too tightly – they will be unusable. During sewing, separate them from the fabric with a matchstick. Slip it out afterwards.

- When buttons are sewn on, paint the thread with colourless nail varnish. Buttons will stay on longer. (This is useful for childrens' or work clothes.)

- Keep buttons on longer with your own button twist. This is how to make it:

  — Thread the needle and pull the thread to make two equal lengths and knot them together at the end.

  — Holding the knot, rub along the thread 3 times with a piece of beeswax.

  — Hold the knot between your finger and thumb and stretch the thread across your palm.

  — Rub your other hand palm downwards, across the hand holding the thread from fingertips to wrist.

— When the thread twists, move the twisted section along (wind it round your thumb).

— Continue until all the thread is done. A piece of thread 100-120 cm/46-48 in. long will be enough for three small or two large buttons. The wax keeps the strands together and makes the thread stronger. Prepare several needles in advance.

Maintenance

- Darn thin patches *before* they wear into holes.

- Darn *first* before washing, or holes will stretch.

- Press darn with a damp cloth or steam iron.

- To remove fluff from clothes, wrap adhesive tape sticky side out round your hand. This will pick up fluff, hair etc from dark material when you brush your hands over it.

Mending tips

- If you are working with slippery fabric, use a cake of soap as a pincushion; it gives the pins better grip.

- Store cotton reels on old knitting needles or barbecue skewers with a cork protecting the sharp end. You can colour code them in any way that suits your sewing priorities.

- Keep a magnet in your sewing box to round up stray pins and needles.

Sheepskin

- Freshen up sheepskin coats with dry shampoo, lightly rubbed into the woolly side. Leave for an hour, shake and brush out (out of doors if possible).

Socks

- Dab socks stained with shoe polish with methylated spirit before laundering (NOT if they are nylon).

- Ultra grubby sports socks should be soaked first in a biological detergent solution or Stain Devils Stain-salts added to the washing water.

- If you are handwashing grubby white socks, add a pinch of bicarbonate of soda to the wash and a few drops of lemon juice to the rinse.

Stockings/tights

- Prolong the life of your tights and stockings. Rinse in warm water, wring out gently, put them in a plastic bag and secure. Leave them overnight in your freezer or icemaking compartment of the fridge. Thaw out next day.

- Don't be too eager to throw away old tights and stockings. They have many uses.

Storage

- Hang dark coloured skirts inside out to prevent dust gathering on them.

- When you take clothes off, hang them up outside your wardrobe for a couple of hours to air.

- Prevent clothes slipping from wooden hangers by sticking a strip of foam rubber on each shoulder of the hanger.

- Allow wet raincoats to dry off before you brush off the mud, otherwise you will spread the dirt.

- Empty pockets, do up zips, buttons and Velcro openings before hanging up clothes. This will help to keep their shape.

- Rescue tired crushed velvet by hanging the garment in a steamy atmosphere (the bathroom while you run a bath for example).

- Separate winter and summer clothes and store out of season garments in a soft plastic wardrobe box which can be stored under the bed or in a warm dry attic.

- Don't waste time folding up shirts or blouses. Hang them on hangers directly after ironing.

- Fold clothes crosswise not lengthwise; the folds drop out quicker.

- Roll up man-made fabrics, rather than folding them. They crease less.

- When packing or storing for the winter, fold clothes over rolled-up plastic bags. These are more resilient than tissue paper and prevent creases.

- For long dresses, sew loops at waist level inside. Turn the bodice to hang over the skirt and attach the dress to hanger with loops. This will keep the hem free from dust.

Zips

- To repair zips at the base, pull slide down below broken teeth. Cut out the teeth. Run slide above the gap, engaging the teeth. Stitch the zip together just above broken part.

- Sew zips onto inside jacket pockets of children's clothes, to prevent losses.

- If a zip sticks, rub the teeth with a soft lead pencil or silicone furniture polish.

BLANKETS

Although most new blankets are permanently mothproofed, old or inherited ones may need to be treated.

- Wash and mothproof woollen blankets in one operation. Make a mixture of

    37.5 ml/3 dessert sps. eucalyptus oil

    250 ml/breakfast cup methylated spirit

    225 g/8 oz soap flakes

    in a screw top jar. Shake until dissolved. Add 15 ml/ 1 tbsp of the mixture to each 4.5 l/1 gallon warm water. Soak blankets until clean. DO NOT RINSE. Spin dry or wring. Dry in fresh air.

    The eucalyptus oil deters moths and replaces lost natural oil. (The smell soon disperses.)

- Blankets that can be washed in the washing machine will benefit from 5 ml/1 tsp olive oil in the final rinse. (This will not mothproof.)

- Synthetic blankets benefit from the use of fabric conditioner.

CURTAINS AND LINENS

- To prevent creasing nylon or Terylene curtains, fold them up before washing. Soak them while still folded to get rid of dust. Wash and rinse still folded, do not crumple them up. Drip dry and hang at the window while still slightly damp.

Drying

- To dry sheets, fold into 4 when wet and peg out with 3 pegs. This will make them easier to iron.

- Dry candlewick bedspreads on the line fluffy side inside on a windy day if possible. This will bring up the pile.

Ironing

- When ironing large sheets or curtains spread an old sheet or large towel on the floor under the ironing board to stop them getting dirty.

General maintenance

- Dust curtains and upholstery regularly using the suction nozzle of the vacuum cleaner. This cuts down the need for more thorough cleaning.

- On a breezy day, hang out curtains to air and freshen.

- Fabrics can be weakened by pollution in the atmosphere and by sunshine. Therefore always make sure that curtains are lined.

- When making curtains, do not hem them straight-away. Hang them for a week or so until their weight settles. The subsequent hemline is less likely to drop.

- When you wash curtains made from material that may shrink, unpick the hems first. When they have been washed, hang them up and wait for them to 'drop' before taking up the hem. If they have shrunk you will be able to iron out the old hemline.

Storage

- Store freshly cleaned curtains folded, linings outwards, on a clamp-style skirt or trouser hanger. This will prevent creasing.

- Mark large sheets (D for double, K for king-size, or your own code) to prevent wasting time getting the wrong sheets out and having to fold them up again.

- Do not store white or light coloured linens in the airing cupboard. They will go yellow.

DUVETS

- Put duvet covers on inside out. Put one hand into a top corner of the cover and grab the top corner of the duvet. Pull through as far as possible. Repeat with other top corner. Shake the duvet cover down.

- Close duvet cover openings before washing and drying, otherwise smaller garments will get trapped and knotted up inside them.

- Dry duvets inside out on the line to prevent the pattern fading.

LINENS

- Dishtowels can be efficiently sterilised in your microwave. Place them on a kitchen towel in the oven. Switch the oven onto high for 5 minutes. DO NOT LEAVE THE MICROWAVE UNATTENDED DURING THIS OPERATION.

UPHOLSTERY

- Dust upholstered items once a week, using the soft brush attachment of the vacuum cleaner. Use the crevice tool around the seat edges.

- Loosen embedded dust by beating furniture with a short cane.

- Turn reversible cushions once a week.

- Keep upholstered furniture out of the sunlight if possible.

- Loose covers can be removed for cleaning. Unless labelled 'washable', have them dry cleaned.

- Soak washable covers in cold water first; this loosens a lot of the dirt.

37

- Get rid of shine from hand-rubbing by wiping with a cloth dampened in a solution of warm water (250 ml/½ pint) and 12.5 ml/dessertspoon of vinegar.

- Clean fixed covers with an upholstery shampoo, following manufacturer's instructions. Always test the product first on an inconspicuous section.

- Replace covers while still slightly damp for a snug fit. Iron *in situ* if necessary. Use a cool iron if furniture is foam-filled.

- To stop loose covers slipping or flapping about, fix Velcro strips to the underside of the edges of loose covers and the corresponding parts of the furniture.

3

Around the house

This section is intended to help you with the cleaning, repair and maintenance of areas duplicated around the house: baths, sinks, doors, floors, surfaces, walls and windows; it includes a few DIY tips and a 'First Aid for Homes Kit' (useful tool box for the non-DIYer).

GENERAL HOUSE CLEANING TIPS

- Don't clutter your shelves with unnecessary one-job proprietary treatments. Bleach, washing-up liquid, washing soda and general purpose cream cleaner are all very versatile.

- Clean lightly and often, rather than heavily twice a year. Accumulated dirt is much harder to shift than a couple of days' dust.

- Take the time to make yourself a cleaning routine and try to stick to it.

- Train your household (and yourself) to put things away not just down. Clutter makes a room look dirty, even though it may not be and wastes a lot of time.

- Carry all your cleaning materials with you in a basket. (Use a shopper on wheels if you live in a flat/ bungalow or have trouble lifting things.)

- Make your own polishing cloth for wood surfaces. Put one eggcupful of vinegar and one of paraffin in a screwtop jar. Stuff a clean duster into the jar, screw on the lid and leave overnight. The duster will absorb the liquid and transform itself into a polisher.

- Empty your vacuum cleaner regularly and do not try to economise by re-using the lining bags. Vacuum cleaners need air to function properly and re-used bags gradually become less porous and impede the air flow.

- Do not throw tea leaves onto a carpet to clean it. Mistresses of the house did this to make sure that the carpet was completely swept by the maid, not because of any secret cleaning ingredient in tea.

- When spring cleaning, start at the top of the house (or back of the flat) and work down (or forward) ending at the front door.

- Do not despise the broom and duster. You can save time, energy and money sweeping up as much dust and dirt as possible (or dusting it off) before attacking with a vacuum cleaner, soap and water or cleaning materials.

Baths and sinks

- Prevent a greasy 'tidemark' forming (especially in hard water areas) by adding a little washing-up liquid to the bathwater. (It is only bubble bath without the scent.)

- Always run cold water in the bath first. This is safer and prevents the bathroom steaming up.

- Restore a dirty and neglected bath by running it full of very hot water. Add a few cupfuls of washing soda. Allow to soak for a couple of hours, longer if necessary. Rub down afterwards.

- Use a hand-held shower to rinse out the bath.

- Clean out the overflow with an old toothbrush dipped in disinfectant.

- For acrylic baths, treat scratches by rubbing with silver metal polish. Deeper gouges can be rubbed down with progressively finer grades of wet-and-dry sandpaper, used wet.

- Clean behind the bath taps with an old toothbrush dipped in bath cleaner.

- Fill the sink with water as hot as your hand can bear. Add some bleach. Wearing rubber gloves plunge your hand in, take out the plug and put it back upside down. The water will flow out slowly, cleaning the overflow, plughole and underside of plug.

- Clear a sink blocked with fat by pouring down very hot water from the kettle. Periodically sluice down with a pail of hot water with a handful of washing soda dissolved in it to prevent grease build up in the drainpipe.

- Polish up stainless steel sinks and drainers with a wad of slightly damp, crumpled newspapers.

Brass

- Treat neglected brass with a strong ammonia solution before cleaning.

- Lemon juice (a couple of squirts) with the brass polish will help keep brass bright and clean for longer.

- When brass is new or newly cleaned, save yourself frequent cleaning by painting on a layer of clear polyurethane varnish, or clear lacquer. (Use a spray for fiddly ornaments.)

- When polishing brass door furniture, make a cardboard collar to protect the door from stray brass polish, which would otherwise bleach the wood over a period of time.

Carpets

- When shampooing carpets, lay strips of foil under heavy pieces of furniture that cannot be moved to prevent marking. Place them directly under feet or under castors.

- Raise small patches of squashed pile by steaming. Lay a damp white cloth over the patch and press gently with a hot iron. When the cloth is dry, remove it and brush up the pile with a stiff brush.

- Always vacuum thoroughly *before* and after shampooing. Vacuum the underside of rugs and small moveable carpets.

- When shampooing, take care not to overwet, or colour may come through from the back.

- Never scrub carpets – the pile will distort and appear a different colour.

- When choosing carpet remember that the more tufts there are per sq. cm/in., the harder wearing it will be. Go for a short, dense pile if the carpet will be subject to heavy traffic.

- When cleaning berber or shagpile rugs or carpets, always use a suction nozzle, never a revolving brush type cleaner which will pull out the strands. If you have lots of 'long-pile' carpets, invest in a carpet rake (from carpet shops).

- If your carpet is regularly trampled, have it treated with a protective spray such as Scotchgard. This is best done professionally (see Addresses). It is a truth generally acknowledged by carpet manufacturers that such treatment is best applied during the manufacturing process rather than afterwards. It is a good idea to choose a carpet protected in this way for areas of heavy traffic. Protected carpets will be labelled to indicate this.

- Remove dents made by heavy furniture from carpets by placing small ice cubes in the dents to melt. This is very successful with wool carpets. Go over with the suction nozzle of the vacuum cleaner when dry to bring up the pile.

- Reduce static on man-made carpets by spraying with a solution of 60 ml/4 tbsp water and 15 ml/1 tbsp fabric softener. Decant into a plant mister before using.

- As static is usually the result of dry conditions caused by central heating, you can get rid of it by increasing the humidity. Keep vases or bowls of water in the room, or you can fit your radiators with humidifiers.

- Remove chewing gum from carpets by scraping off as much as possible with a spoon, then pressing a polythene bag containing ice-cubes on the remainder. Frozen chewing gum becomes brittle and is easy to break away.

- Trim unmoveable lumps of chewing gum from carpet tufts with nail scissors.

- Slight scorching can often be removed by rubbing with the cut surface of a raw onion.

- Pick up cotton bits from carpet with damp sponge or foam rubber or wear rubber gloves and pick them up with your fingers.

- To cure an old rug from curling upwards, take it up and coat the back with glue size. Leave to dry. DO NOT DO THIS TO ANTIQUE OR VALUABLE ITEMS.

- Never polish the floor underneath rugs or mats.

- To stop rugs slipping, brush several strips of latex adhesive across the back. Allow to dry thoroughly before putting down.

- To keep a rug in place on a carpet, glue a strip of Velcro Anti-Creep or foam rubber to the sides and corners.

- Jampot washers sewn on each corner will hold small rugs in place on carpets.

- To anchor a precious antique rug, do not glue foam rubber on, but lay the rug on a piece of foam rubber cut to the correct size.

- Make a neat join between two carpets in a doorway with an aluminium gripper strip.

- When estimating for stair carpet, allow an extra amount (enough to cover a stair tread and riser). Then you can move the carpet occasionally to prevent bald patches on the stair edges.

- Buy cheap carpet samples and use them as doormats.

- Use leftover carpet tiles as a rest for typewriter or sewing machines.

Chrome

- Remove corrosion from chrome with a 1:1 solution of household ammonia and water. Paraffin or tooth-paste on a damp cloth make excellent substitutes if you don't have any ammonia.

- Hardwater deposits around the taps can be removed by rubbing with a paste of salt and vinegar or vinegar and ground white chalk. Rub up with dry chamois leather.

- Get rid of stains and grease marks with a damp sponge dipped in bicarbonate of soda.

Condensation

- Avoid condensation on bathroom mirrors and windows by rubbing over with a little neat washing-up liquid. Polish off with a sheet of kitchen paper.

Cookers/ovens

- Unless your oven is self-cleaning, it will need periodic cleaning. Put the oven on a moderate heat for 20 minutes. Switch off, place an overproof bowl of strong household ammonia on the top shelf and a dish of boiling water on the bottom. Close the door and leave overnight. In the morning, take out and discard the ammonia and water, and clean the oven with a washing-up liquid solution.

- Sponge oven walls with a solution of bicarbonate of soda and water. Turn oven on low for 20 minutes and allow to cool. Use washing-up liquid and water solution to rinse off the walls. Wipe with a cloth wrung out in the bicarbonate solution and leave to dry. This leaves a grease absorbing layer which makes subsequent cleaning easier.

- Never use cream cleaner on halogen hobs as it leaves a film. Always follow the instructions provided by the manufacturer and clean with their recommended product.

- Never line the grill pan or any other part of the cooker with aluminium foil. It is a serious fire risk.

Copper

- Make your own copper cleaner. Mix together two egg whites, pinch of salt, small glass of vinegar and four soup spoons of plain flour. Rub the mixture on copper pans, kettles etc. Rinse in warm water and polish dry.

- A half lemon dipped in salt, or a salt and vinegar paste can also shift stains. Rinse immediately and dry with a soft cloth.

Doors

- Invest in a good thick doormat. Research indicates up to 80 per cent of dirt and dust can be kept out of the house by a robust mat.

- When choosing a draught excluder for doors, bear in mind what is on the floor. If the door opens onto carpet, a brush-style excluder is best, a rigid metal one may make the door jam.

- Cure creaking doors by oiling hinges from the top with a lubricant such as 3-in-One oil. Be sparing and wipe off any surplus.

- Fit safety glass to interior glazed doors, french doors, patio doors and glazed panels in front doors.

- Alternatively, cover with shrink-on safety film. This will also afford a small degree of insulation.

- If your doors stick, there could be a number of reasons:

  - Paint build-up (usually old doors) – the door and frame must be stripped off.

  - New carpet (higher pile) – the door will need to be removed from the frame and planed down or fitted with rising butt hinges to lift it as it opens.

  - Damp causes wood to swell and jam – the door will have to be removed from its hinges and planed down. Remember that the wood may shrink back in warm weather, so do not plane over-enthusiastically.

  - Worn hinges – sometimes swapping top and bottom hinges can help; otherwise new ones should be fitted.

- Never fit locks to internal doors that form a fire escape route.

- Protect door knobs with kitchen foil when painting doors. This will allow you to open them while you work.

Lavatories

- Use lavatory cleaner last thing at night; this allows the lavatory bowl to 'soak' for a longer period than in the daytime.

- Rinse the lavatory brush in a mild disinfectant solution at regular intervals.

- Never mix bleach with other lavatory cleaners (powder, cream or liquid). Poisonous chlorine gas could result.

Marble surfaces

- Remove stains by trickling on lemon juice. Rinse off quickly.

- Colourless wax can be applied to coloured marble to add shine, but not to white as it can cause yellowing.

- Repolish shiny marble with chamois leather and whiting (available from artist's materials suppliers).

- To rejuvenate grimy marble, paint the surface with a compound of 1 part powdered pumice, 1 part powdered chalk and 2 parts bicarbonate of soda mixed to a paste with a little water. Leave the paste on overnight. Wash off with clean water and a soft nail brush.

Plastic laminate surfaces

- Print/ink stains from packages on damp surfaces can sometimes be removed with lemon juice.

- Tea and coffee stains can be dissolved with a solution of washing soda.

Radiators

- To clean old fashioned radiators, hang a damp towel behind then blow through with vacuum nozzle or hair dryer. The dust will collect neatly on the towel.

- Fit a shelf above a radiator to prevent discolouration made by dust rising in the hot air currents.

Sinks (*See* BATHS AND SINKS)

Showers

- Clean blocked shower heads with a proprietary shower head cleaner on a toothbrush or by removing it and boiling in a vinegar solution.

- Wash soap deposits from shower curtains by soaking in warm water in which you have dissolved 30 ml/2 tbsp fabric conditioner. Rinse; wipe dry.

- Scrub mildewed shower curtains with a paste of bicarbonate of soda and water. Rinse off. Alternatively, sponge them down with a mild bleach solution.

- Soak new shower curtains in salt water solution to prevent mildew developing.

- Clean water marks from glass shower doors with neat vinegar on a cloth.

FLOORS

General tips

- Vacuum or sweep up dust first. Clean with a damp, rather than soaking wet, mop, using 2 buckets of water (one to clean and one for rinsing).

- Do not use a bleach solution with a cellulose mop as it will disintegrate.

- Before using an electric polisher, dust the floor, otherwise the machine will efficiently grind the dirt into the floor with the polish.

Ceramic floors

- Do not polish ceramic tiles, you will make them dangerously slippery.

Concrete floors

- Keep down dust by painting with 2 coats of a mixture of PVA adhesive and water (1 part adhesive to 5 parts water).

Cork floors

- Do not overwet cork tiles, as they will lift.

- If the cork is unsealed, polish with non-slip wax polish.

Linoleum floors

- Repair cracks in linoleum with adhesive tape. Paint over the tape with a coat of clear polyurethane varnish.

Loose floorboards

- Drive down nails with hammer and nail punch. If this does not work, drill holes next to the nails and fix the boards to joists with countersunk screws.

Quarry tiles

- Remove white patches by mopping with a weak solution 60 ml/4 tbsp vinegar in 4.5 l/1 gallon water. Leave to dry without rinsing. Repeat if necessary. Do not polish until the patches stop appearing.

Vinyl

- Do not use alkaline floor cleaners on vinyl (for instance, borax, washing soda solution, or soap-based liquid solution); they can take out plasticisers from vinyl, leading to shrinkage, brittleness and cracking. Use warm water with a few drops of washing-up liquid and rinse finally with clear water containing a dash of vinegar.

- Remove marks on sheet vinyl or tiles with a clean india rubber.

- Remove heel marks on light coloured vinyl floors with white spirit or turpentine on a cloth. Wash over at once with soapy water.

- Use a rubber headed car brush to clean vinyl or rubber floors. The flexible bristles are flexible enough to get into corners and round pipes.

Woodblock floors

- Sweep often as grit can cause damage.

- Never overwet, as it causes warping.

- Remove stubborn marks with fine steel wool.

WALLS AND CEILINGS

- When washing walls, wash from the *bottom* upwards. Rinse each section in the same way. This prevents streaking, which happens if the dirty water tickles down uncleaned sections.

- Remove stubborn stains with neat washing-up liquid or household cleaner. Rinse well.

- Do not paint over polystyrene ceiling tiles. This could prove a fire hazard.

- Scrub soot from stone or brick walls with clear water and a fibre (not wire) scrubbing brush.

Ceramic tiles

- Dissolve limescale by wiping with neat vinegar. Use a proprietary acid based cleaner specially designed for the job if stains are stubborn. (Follow manufacturer's instructions.)

- Refresh dingy grouting by scrubbing gently with a bleach solution (cover floor and surroundings to prevent damage). If you find mould stains, you may need a proprietary fungicidal cleaner.

- When drilling into ceramic tiles, stick a patch of masking tape on the spot where you want to drill.

- To remove one damaged tile, first scrape out grouting. Drill hole in centre of tile or score with a tile cutter. Chip out debris and tile with cold chisel. (Wear goggles.) Scrape out old adhesive. Then follow instructions for the new glue before replacing the tile.

- Use matchsticks as separators when fixing new tiles.

- When buying tiles, allow a few extras for repairs.

Wallpaper

- Remove grease spots by laying a piece of blotting paper over the spot and pressing with a warm iron.

- General dirt and grime can be rubbed off wallpaper with a wedge of white bread.

- Tie string across a paste bucket to make a rest for the brush. You can also use it to scrape off overload. (This also works for paintbrushes.)

- Patch wallpaper with a torn rather than cut out piece. Remove the stained or damaged part by spraying with water and gently pulling it off. Paste the new patch on the wall. The feathered edges will blend in more successfully than a straight cut piece.

- Do not hang vinyl wallpaper near a cooker. Heat and splashes of fat or oil could damage it.

- To prepare wallpaper for stripping use a paint roller dipped in a solution of hot water and washing-up liquid.

- Make your own device for papering behind radiators. Bind a strip of rag around a wire coathanger to pad it. Attach the coat hanger to a wooden handle.

- Leave surplus trimmings (around light switches, ceiling roses etc) for 24 hours before cutting them off. It will be easier to trim when the paste is dry.

WINDOWS

- To wash windows, add a few drops of household ammonia or 30 ml/2 tbsp vinegar to a bucket of clear water. Apply with sponge or cloth. Remove with a rubber window-cleaning blade. Polish with spray cleaner if necessary and a soft cloth or scrunched-up newspapers.

- Clean windows on a dull day. Sunlight dries windows too quickly, leaving smears on glass.

- Condensation can be prevented by rubbing window glass with neat washing-up liquid on a dry cloth.

- Leave upper windows to professionals.

- The best way to get a shine on windows is to polish them with scrunched up old newspapers. The newsprint prevents smearing.

- Prevent rust on metal curtain tracks and make running smoother by spraying lightly with an aerosol lubricant such as WD 40.

- Keep double glazing tracks smooth by spraying with silicone furniture polish. (Choose ozone friendly spray.)

Double glazing

- Cheap temporary double glazing can be made with kits or shrink-on polythene film. Use a hair dryer on coolest setting to 'set' the film. Peel it off at the end of winter and repeat the following year.

- If you do have double glazing, make sure that there is a removable section in each unit large enough for an adult to climb through in case of fire.

Maintenance

- When handling sheets of glass or working with broken glass, wear thick gloves.

- Never use a blowlamp to strip paint from window frames and glazing bars, as heat will crack the glass.

- Remove fitments such as handles before painting windows. Alternatively, mask them with masking tape, newspaper or kitchen foil (useful for casement handles).

- Do not paint windows when closed. They may never open again.

- Stop paint spattering onto glass by sticking decorator's masking tape next to the glazing bars. You can remove any residue of adhesive when you have peeled off the tape with a rag dampened with lighter fuel.

- Remember that you should allow a certain amount of paint to glide over the putty to help keep it in place.

- Remove rust from metal windows with a chemical rust remover. Wear goggles and gloves and make sure none gets onto your skin. Brush off as much rust, dirt and grease as possible. Apply rust remover with an old paintbrush and leave to work for 10-15 minutes. Follow manufacturer's instructions.

- Cure rattling sash windows temporarily by inserting plastic wedges or wads of cardboard to keep the sashes firmly in place. (Repairs are quite difficult for a non-DIYer.)

- If a window has become 'painted-up', prise the window and its frame apart by wedging a thin wallpaper scraper between them and tapping the handle lightly. When the paint has given, open the window. Push the window up and down or in and out. Smooth off the sides and frame of the window with glasspaper.

Roller blinds

- If your roller blind will not stay down, it may need lubricating. Remove it from its brackets and hold it upright with the spring mechanism uppermost. Lay a paper towel over the blind fabric and spray the mechanism bar with an aerosol lubricant (only a short burst). Allow the lubricant to soak inside the mechanism. Clean and lubricate the wall brackets before remounting the blind.

- If your new roller blind will not roll up and down correctly, check the following:

  — Are the brackets level?

  — Is the material absolutely square? (Especially if it is a home-made blind.)

- To correct tension, remove blind from brackets and wind up spring mechanism (square piece of metal on the left hand of the roller). Turn it a few times, hold it firmly to prevent unwinding and replace blind. Pull the blind down and let it up slowly a few times until the action is smooth.

Venetian blinds

- Wash venetian blinds *in situ* by putting on strong fabric gloves, plunging your hands in a hot solution of washing-up liquid and drawing each slat through your gloved fingers. Rinse in the same manner.

- For a spring clean, or if they are very greasy, take the blinds down and give them a bath. Lay on old towel on the bath bottom, and fill the bath with a mild solution of washing-up liquid. Avoid getting the blind mechanisms wet. Rinse in the same manner. Wipe off excess water and rehang. Leave the blinds in the down position until dry.

- Keep Venetian blinds cleaner for longer by polishing them with anti-static polish.

PAINTING AND DECORATING

- Cut an onion in half and put it cut sides up in a room while you are painting. This will dispel unpleasant odours.

- With gloss and aerosol paint, it is better to apply 2 or 3 thin, light coats than one thick one. Thin gloss paint with white spirit.

- Protect door handles with kitchen foil while you paint. That way you will be able to use them during decorating.

- To stop skin forming on gloss paint, pour a thin layer of white spirit on top before closing the tin.

- When painting glazing bars, protect the window glass by sticking strips of decorator's masking tape alongside the bars. Leave a millimetre or so. A little paint along the putty line helps keep the window pane in.

- Alternatively, smear petroleum jelly around the edges of the window pane. At the end of the job, you will be able to wipe off the jelly and any paint with it very easily.

- When choosing paint, look at the sample cards in the light of the room they will be in. Different light changes the paint shade.

- Drill a hole in the paintbrush handle (some have them already). Then you can thread it onto a dowel or nail and suspend the brush in cleaning fluid without bristles getting pushed out of shape on the bottom.

- Wrap your brush tightly in foil or clingfilm while you break off for lunch or overnight. This saves the bother of cleaning it every time you stop.

- When painting with a roller, cover the tray with foil first. After the job this can be peeled off and thrown away, leaving the roller tray clean.

- Strain lumpy paint through old tights or stockings.

- Stand paint tins on paper plates (larger than the tin). This will catch drips most efficiently.

- After cleaning with white spirit (gloss) or soapy water (emulsion), hang brushes up to dry. Flick bristles to shake out loose ones and remove dust. Store brushes flat.

- Clean your hands with cooking oil after a painting session. Rub hands hard with oil (about 5 ml/1 tsp), then wipe with a towel. Your hands will be clean and soft, not dry and cracked as with white spirit.

A simple tool kit

Below are listed a few essential tools for small jobs around the home. Keep them separate from your electrical kit (see page 93).

- Claw hammer (for pulling out nails)

- Pin-head hammer (for tacks and pins)

- Selection of flat blade screwdrivers (small, medium)

- Cross head Phillips screwdriver

- Pair of pliers

- Pair of pincers

- Stanley knife and spare blades

- Selection of wet-and-dry sandpaper (various grades)

- General purpose panel saw

- Surform rasp (for rough rubbing down of wood)

- Goggles

- Face masks (available in multipacks of disposables)

- 3-in-1 oil

- A selection of screws, nails, panel pins and tacks kept in small screw-top jars. (Label them.) Then you can see what you have left

- An oilstone (for sharpening knives and tools)

- Tape measure (extending metal tape)

- Spirit level

- 5 m/5 yard extension cable which rewinds into its case

- Choose tools yourself when buying. They should be the right weight for *you*.

- Rewind extension leads after use to avoid trailing flexes and damage. Check for damage/cuts. If you find any replace the cable. *DO NOT MEND WITH INSULATING TAPE*

- Sharpen chisels, knives and planes on oilstone after each use.

- If tools are kept in the shed or garage, wipe the metal parts with a rag dipped in light lubricating oil before putting them away after a job.

- Rub the head of your hammer with sandpaper to give good grip.

- Don't forget to put strips of masking tape over the spot when drilling into ceramic tiles.

- Rub screws with soap, petroleum jelly or candle-grease before driving in, to make entry and removal easier.

- Push tacks through a piece of paper before hammering into the surface. Use the paper to help you position the tack. Hold the paper, not the tack, while hammering. (Saves thumbs.)

- Loosen a tight screw by dribbling vinegar onto the screw head. It will run down the thread and make it easier to unscrew.

- Chisel out build up of paint in a screw slot with an old screwdriver and hammer.

4

Pests and infestations

Wall-to-wall carpeting, central heating, the popularity of indoor plants and the enormous dog and cat population have all encouraged the proliferation of household pests. Below are listed some of the more common horrors, with some ideas on how to cope. Always use ozone-friendly, CFC-free aerosols. Before you go on a seek and destroy mission, consider whether it is essential to wipe out all of the insects. Flies, bluebottles and cockroaches are all disease vectors as are mice and rats; but ants, wasps and bees are a positive help, as they eat other pests. Try to strike an ecological balance.

You need have no such scruples about rot and mould. Urgent professional help is essential.

Ants

- Consider whether you need to do anything. Black ants are very useful in destroying other pests and are generally harmless to humans.

- Find the nest (this is usually outside) and pour boiling water into it.

- Put down poisonous ant-bait, which the ants take back into the nest themselves. Don't use this if you have pets or children.

- Keep ants out of the kitchen by 'drawing' a barrier with one of the pen-type insecticides (eg Vapona Insectipen). Then the ants can get on with their lives in the garden.

- Essence of peppermint poured into the nest will discourage ants.

Bees and wasps

Try not to destroy these insects. They are harmless unless provoked and wasps are very useful predators of insects more harmful to mankind.

- Try to restore bees to the garden. If they are buzzing against the window, place a glass or jar against the pane, trapping the insect. Slide a sheet of paper between glass or jar rim and the window. Then you can carry the bee outside and release it.

- If you are besieged by wasps, line your window sills with wasp-traps made from jars filled with a mixture of water, detergent and jam/marmalade/honey. They will attract and drown the wasps.

- If you come across a swarm, call your local Environmental Health Officer immediately. Do not try to move the swarm yourself.

Carpet beetle

These are fast taking over from moths as textile pests. They are brown and cream ladybird-like insects about 4 mm/¹⁄₁₆ in. long, which look like a furry coffee bean. The larvae cause the trouble, as they eat the wool, carpet etc. when they hatch. Carpet beetles are found in pipe lagging, airing cupboards and carpet fluff. They live on fur, feathers and wool fluff, and breed in bird's nests. To eliminate them:

- Find the source (usually loft or eaves). Vacuum well, spray with CFC-free aerosol moth proofer. This also works on carpets and textiles but test first on an insignificant area.

- If stored blankets or woollen jumpers are affected, wash or dry clean, then store with a cotton bag of paradichlorbenzene crystals (available from chemists or herbalists). Better still, use a proprietary moth-proofer. Most do not have a lingering smell.

- Never spray fur coats infested with carpet beetle. Have them treated professionally.

Cockroaches

- These insects (dark brown, about 25 mm/1 in. long) carry diseases that affect humans (polio, dysentery, typhoid), which is spread by their excrement. They also smell unpleasant.

- If you have an infestation, clean everything thoroughly and cover all food. Use small-space fly killer, a Vapona Insectipen barrier, if you can find the cockroaches entry point, or ant and crawling insect aerosol. Choose a CFC-free variety eg Raid.

- If the cockroaches are out of control, contact your local Pest Control Office.

Earwigs

- These are plant-loving insects, so make sure all tendrils and creepers are kept away from doors and windows. Treat outside door thresholds, window-sills and airbricks with a garden powder insecticide.

- Keep leaves and bark away from the house. Barrier insecticides (eg Vapona Insectipen) can help keep earwigs from the kitchen.

Fleas

These are usually spread from cats or dogs and are most prevalent in the summer.

- Treat the animal(s) following veterinary advice with CFC-free flea spray.

- Treat the carpet (including the underneath edges) and affected furnishings. Follow the instructions. *Do not spray foam backing on carpets or rugs.*

- Vacuum all areas 24 hours later to clear away dead fleas and eggs.

- Repeat if necessary.

Flies

Flies and bluebottles spread disease and should be excluded from the kitchen.

- Choose CFC-free aerosol such as Raid.

- As aerosol insecticides can affect pets and people as well as flies, choose a slow-release fly killer (eg Vapona) place out of the reach of children and away from food.

- Old fashioned sticky fly-papers are now available once more.

- Barrier insecticides (eg Vapona Insectipen) drawn across door thresholds, windows and along any cracks will help keep out flies.

- On sunny days, keep the windows on the sunny side of the house/flat closed; that's the way flies come in.

- Bead curtains are very efficient at keeping flies out of localised areas.

Greenfly and Whitefly (see pages 121, 122)

Mice and rats

- Mice are attracted by food, so keep all food products wrapped up and stored away and tidy up crumbs and dropped food immediately.

- Find the mouse holes and put down dishes of turpentine or peppermint which mice find repellent.

- Mouse poison is not successful for long, as mice breed quickly and develop immunity. The best deterrent for mice is a cat.

- If you are infested by rats you must inform the Environmental Health Officer.

Moths

You will know that moths have laid eggs in your woollens when the larvae hatch, eat their fill and leave tiny holes in wool, and bald patches on furs and, surprisingly, holes in wine bottle corks.

- Check for moths in airing cupboards, drawers and wardrobes. They prefer warm and undisturbed conditions.

- To prevent infestation, spray freshly cleaned clothes/ blankets with CFC-free aerosol moth repellent. Test on an insignificant section first.

- Store the sprayed article wrapped in brown paper and packed in a strong plastic bag.

- Alternatively, leave a slow release moth repellent strip in drawers or wardrobes.

- To avoid chemicals, try an old herbal remedy. Hang a bunch of fresh thyme in the wardrobe. As it dries out, it inhibits moth infestation.

Psocids

These are tiny (just over 1 mm/$\frac{1}{24}$ in.) grey insects that infest food cupboards.

- Empty and thoroughly clean out the cupboard. Discard affected food products.

- Treat with an insecticide.

- Try to find another place for storing food; use the space to store tins and secure packets only.

- Keep all food cupboards well ventilated, as a warm humid atmosphere attracts all sorts of insect pests.

Silverfish

These are small wingless insects with silvery scales about 13 mm/½ in. long, with three bristly tails. They are slow breeders.

- Silverfish thrive in damp conditions and live on starch products (including wallpaper glue and book-binding glue); they are harmless.

- Eliminate damp; this will discourage them; likewise don't leave crumbs lying about.

- Sprinkle a little of a mixture of sugar and borax (1:1) if you want to get rid of them (but not if you have young children in the house).

Woodlice

- Remember that woodlice *prefer* life in the garden. Look for their colony site (usually under logs, or rock piles) and move it further away.

- Keep piles of leaves, bark, stones etc. away from house doors.

- Draw a barrier with an insecticide pen (eg Vapona Insectipen) to discourage the woodlice.

- Lure them into a humane trap. A peeled baked potato in a flower pot will entice the surrounding woodlice population. Then you can move the pot to a new site.

Woodworm (Anobium Punctatum) and similar insects

- Always inspect second-hand furniture for wood-worm before allowing it into your house. Wood-worm can spread to other pieces.

- Look for small, pin-sized holes (about 1.5 mm/$\frac{1}{16}$ in.) surrounded by fine fresh sawdust or sawdust on the floor under furniture. If you find any, call in expert help immediately.

- Death Watch beetle (*Xestobium Rufovillosum*). These beetles prefer old decayed timber and usually con-gregate in the roof timbers of old houses. The exit holes the hatched larvae make are about 3 mm/$\frac{1}{8}$ in. in diameter, twice the size of woodworm holes.

- Powder Post beetle (*Lyctus Brunneus* and *L. Lin-nearis*). These beetles are usually found in timber warehouses, but occasionally appear in domestic woodwork. They prefer hardwood, particularly par-quet flooring. They leave holes like woodworm holes, but the dust is more floury.

- House Longhorn beetle (*Hylotrupes Bajalus*). These may be confused with woodworm, as they leaves similar holes. They live in seasoned softwood (pine, deal) and can remain and can remain dormant for up to 11 years.

In all cases when you find tell-tale holes, call in professional help.

ROT AND MOULD

Dry rot

- Dry rot thrives in still air. Do not block off airbricks. Look for dry rot in door and window frames, floor-boards, skirting boards and wooden stairs.

- To test for dry rot, poke suspected area with a sharp tool (eg a metal skewer) every few feet. If the blade sinks in easily, and the wood feels spongy and soft, suspect the worst. Send for professional help quickly. Dry rot splits wood along and across the grain, making it easily recognisable.

- Burn any infected wood immediately (once it has been hacked out).

Wet rot

- This affects very wet timber, so is most often found in very damp basements or chronically leaking roofs. It is recognised by its pattern of splitting wood along the grain. You will need professional help.

- With both wet and dry rot, check surrounding wood carefully, and eliminate the conditions (damp, leaks, lack of ventilation) that encouraged rot in the first place. Burn decayed wood.

Mould

- Mould is the result of condensation. Do not be too zealous when insulating your house. Leave some air inlets so that the fabric of the building can breathe.

- Black mould is the result of condensation in the kitchen and/or bathroom. Treat affected areas first then install an extractor fan.

- Open up old chimneys and have them swept.

- To treat mould growth on walls, strip off the wallpaper if necessary, wash the plaster with fungicidal wash or a solution of household bleach. Allow to dry thoroughly. Paint the wall with mould resistant paint. If you want to re-wallpaper, use fungicidal wallpaper paste.

- Treat black mould on windows by washing off the mould and rubbing down the paintwork with a medium grade sandpaper. Gouge out mouldy putty and replace if necessary. When you repaint, allow paint to overlap onto the glass by 3 mm/⅛ in.

5

Working the system

WATERWORKS

Domestic water systems are easier to understand than it may seem at first leak. Even though most important jobs have to be undertaken by professional plumbers, it is a sensible notion to familiarize yourself with the pipe layout and track down the stopcocks and gate valves so that you can turn them off immediately in an emergency.

Water comes into your house through a mains pipe called a rising main. It is controlled by a stopcock, usually found in the cellar, the kitchen or just outside the house. Stopcocks look like large taps. Find out where yours is and keep it in good order. Oil the spindle and test turn it occasionally so that it is guaranteed to respond in an emergency. Outside your house is the Water Authority stopcock (look for a small metal cover with a keyhole).

Householders are responsible for all maintenance and repairs from the Authority stopcock. There are two kinds of system, direct and indirect.

Direct system

Found in older, unmodernised houses. The rising main supplies *all* the cold water – for all the taps, lavatory and a small storage tank. This means that water is drinkable from all taps, but there is a risk of back syphonage of foul water from the lavatory system. It is impossible to run water-filled central heating radiators from a direct system; at peak times the mains pressure may fall, affecting your cold supply; and if there is a shortage, the small storage tank may not hold enough for your immediate needs.

Indirect system

Most modern and renovated houses have this kind of system (some Water Authorities insist on it). In this system the rising main feeds only one (or at the most two) taps to the kitchen supplying the drinking water. The rest goes into the cold storage tank. This is usually in the roof space and will hold about 200 l/50 gallons. Storage tanks should be fitted with lids: this is a byelaw requirement and intrinsically desirable to help prevent freezing and contamination of the water. As the water has been standing for a while, it is not a good idea to drink from taps supplied by the tank.

The tank is fed continuously by the rising main, but the water level is controlled by a *ball valve*. This is an ingenious device, extremely simple, accessible and easy to repair. A lightweight ball floats on the surface of the water; it is attached by a float arm, which is itself attached to a valve covering the main inlet. This valve opens and closes to regulate the supply from the rising main. The ball rises and falls with the water level, causing the float arm to push the valve shut when the tank is full and the level is high, and pull the valve open when water is drained out of the tank and the level falls. The same kind of valve controls water levels in the lavatory cistern, so you can look inside this to get an idea of how it works.

The pipes leading from the cold water tank should be fitted with stopcocks or gate valves. Gate valves have small wheel handles, and allow two-way flow. Keep them lubricated and turnable so that you can isolate the tank if there is any problem with the pipes. The pipe that feeds the hot water tank runs from the bottom of the cold water tank.

Hot water tanks

These are the insulated tanks usually found in the airing cupboard. They are fed from the cold water tank, and supply hot water via a pipe from the top of the tank. There is also an expansion pipe which runs up and over the cold water tank. This accommodates overheated water which can bubble up and vent safely into the cold water tank.

There are two types of hot water tank:

The *direct* tank is really a storage heater for water heated by the boiler or by an immersion element.

The *indirect* tank is more complicated. It is supplied with cold water from the cold tank, which is heated up by an enclosed loop of piping (the calorifier) containing hot water supplied directly from the boiler. The calorifier supplies hot water directly to the radiators, while hot tap water comes from the water in the body of the tank. The calorifier, radiators and boiler have their own water tank called a *header tank*. This holds about 16 1/4 gallons. It is usually sited next to the main cold tank, which feeds it, and its water level is controlled by a ball valve. Check regularly that the valve is working. Press the float arm down as far as it will go and see if the tank fills. If it doesn't, call the plumber. The expansion pipe from the boiler (which accommodates excess overheated water) empties into the header tank.

Lavatories

Lavatories are supplied by mains water on the direct system, which accounts for the eccentric flushing patterns experienced with some elderly lavatories. Most modern lavatories are supplied indirectly from the cold water tank, which fills the cistern. Water level in the cistern is controlled by the ball valve. The hints below are meant to help you cope with small matters and take preventative measures. However you should learn to recognise when you are beaten and when you should call professional help:

— If you cannot find/turn the stopcock and there is a flood or burst pipes.

— When you have turned off everything you can

71

and made first aid repairs (see pages 73, 74).

— If you discover that any part of the system, especially the rising main as this carries the drinking water, is made of lead. Lead pipes should be replaced as soon as possible.

— If the taps have seized up (although you might tackle changing a washer yourself, following instructions as supplied by a reputable book).

PLUMBING

Fighting the freeze

• Keep basin plugs in their holes at night to prevent outlets becoming ice-bound.

• Keep your pipes properly lagged.

• If pipes become frozen, try to thaw them before they crack. Use a hairdryer (on low setting) or towels/cloths wrung out in hot water, or a hot water bottle over a cloth. Work from the tap to the tank. NEVER USE A BLOWLAMP ON AN ELECTRIC HEATER. A blow lamp will crack the pipe, and if water from the thawing pipe falls on the heater you risk an accident.

• Inspect frozen copper pipes carefully, as ice can push the compression joints out of alignment. Loosen the nut on the compression fitting, push the pipe back into the joint, then tighten the nut once more. Check for leaks when the pipe has thawed.

• If the main stopcock is in the house, turn it off at night, so you will not wake up to a nocturnal deluge. If it is outside, keep it (and its access) ice and snow free so you can reach it in a hurry.

• Keep stop taps (stopcocks and gate valves) easy to

turn by oiling the spindle occasionally and testing them for 'turnability' before winter sets in.

- Lag pipes leading to outside taps, or isolate the pipes (turn off gate valve) and drain down. Leave taps open to allow for expansion of any remaining water when it freezes.

- If you are going away for a long period, and the house will be empty, close down the entire system. Turn off the stopcock, turn on all taps to drain the system, drain the lavatory cistern (see page 76). If you have water-filled radiators, drain those as well. (Make sure you know how to do this properly; partially drained radiators will cause big trouble. Check with your plumber/central heating engineer.)

- Outdoor drains that have frozen may be cleared by throwing a handful of kitchen salt over the blockage, followed by a kettleful of boiling water.

- If your lavatory S-bend becomes frozen, wrap the bend in towels wrung out in hot water (lay newspapers under the bend to catch drips.) DO NOT POUR BOILING WATER DIRECTLY INTO THE LAVATORY PAN OR A FIRECLAY SINK. The sudden change of temperature may crack the bowl (which will be worse than a frozen lavatory).

- Unfreeze a frozen ball valve by pouring boiling water over it. Move the pivot arm up and down with care to work it free.

- Unfreeze sink U-traps with hot towels (as above).

Repairing burst pipes

- Try to repair pipes before they thaw.

- Open all taps to drain the system.

- Turn off the central heating boiler and turn off the main stopcock. Isolate the burst by closing gate valves if possible. Look for the affected pipe. If the blockage is not obvious, start at the cold water tank and work outwards.

- Make a temporary repair until you can get hold of a plumber. You can use car body filler. Leave it to set and then bind over the crack with repair tape. Failing that, ordinary bandage and epoxy resin adhesive can be used. Spread adhesive on both the pipe and the bandage. Wrap the bandage round the pipe, adding adhesive as you go. Wear rubber gloves.

- Stand a bucket underneath the pipe if possible, to catch overflow when the ice melts.

- If you are too late to mend the pipe before the thaw and the ceiling is bulging, it is better to drill small holes into the ceiling (working from the room above) than risk the entire ceiling falling down. (Station buckets strategically and move the furniture.)

- If the mains pipe bursts outside the house, beyond the Water Authority stopcock, call the Water Board. You cannot turn off the official stopcock, which controls the supply to several houses. However, you can turn off your own stopcock, usually in the cellar or just outside the house where the supply enters.

NB If the mains burst and you have no water supply, switch off gas or oil-fired boilers, and electric immersion heaters; damp down solid fuel fires which heat the water supply, shovelling out the fuel if necessary (as soon as it is safe to do so).

Repairing leaking pipes

- Trace the pipe back to its feed cistern if possible, and

turn off the stopcock controlling the cistern. If there is no stopcock, turn off the main one.

- Turn off all water heaters. Open all the taps. Turn off the stopcock on the outlet tap or the cold water cistern.

- Check whether you are dealing with copper or lead pipes. Many older properties still have lead supply pipes, and in areas where the water supply is hard this is not a significant problem. (In soft water areas local authorities may give householders grants towards the cost of replacing lead pipes.)

- For copper pipes, try tightening the two large nuts on each side of the join. This may stop the leak.

- If it obviously needs more attention, call your plumber. Meanwhile, make a temporary repair. Wipe the pipe surface and slap over a coat of paint. Bind it with rags and thin strips of polythene. (Cut up old plastic carriers or bin liners.)

- Lead pipes cannot be patched up this way, but may respond to careful tapping with a hammer to close the split (lead is malleable). A plumber is essential in this case.

Cisterns and tanks

Dealing with an overflowing cistern (or water tank).

- If your cistern or water tank is overflowing, check the ball valve.

- Check that the float arm is not set too high. Turn off the water supply. Loosen the nut holding the ball valve in place and move the ball down 1 cm/⅓ in.

- If the ball cannot be moved, use a spanner or pliers to carefully bend the bar down at the ball end. Lower it by 1 cm/⅓ in. DO NOT BEND PLASTIC ARMS.

- The problem may be with the ball. Check to see that the ball is whole. If it is split or corroded and lets in water, it will not work correctly. Unscrew the ball and replace it, preferably with a plastic one (available at DIY stores). NB If the repair is in the water tank ball valve, and going to take more than a few minutes, turn off all water heating.

- The problem may be the inlet valve, which may be worn or dirty. Modern cistern inlet valves are easily replaced. TURN OFF THE WATER SUPPLYING THE CISTERN FIRST. Unscrew the end cap with a pair of grips, fit a new diaphragm. Replace and tighten the screw cap.

- To stop water flowing into the cistern (for example when you are draining down the system), rest a narrow length of wood across the tank. Tie the float arm to the wood. This will automatically shut off the inlet valve and prevent water flowing into the tank while allowing mains water to be used elsewhere in the house.

- As a stop-gap measure, encase a cracked ball in a polythene bag. Make sure it is watertight where it is tied on. This will allow you to use the cistern while waiting for a new ball.

Dealing with an airlock in the system

- If water spurts or sputters out of your tap, stops unaccountably, then bursts out again accompanied by loud knocking sounds, you have an airlock:

    - Mains pressure may be enough to cure this. Fit a short length of hosepipe to connect the cold mains tap and the hot tap in the kitchen sink.

Secure both ends with hoseclips (tighten them up with a screwdriver). Turn on *both* taps (hot first) and let them run for a few minutes. The idea is that mains pressure from the cold tap will force the airlock back through the hot water pipes to bubble out in the hot water tank. Use caution.

— Repeat the exercise, but if you are getting nowhere after 20 minutes or so, or the airlock is recurring, call a plumber.

NB If you have mixer taps in the kitchen you must use another pair of taps for this manoeuvre. As the cold tap must be mains fed, this will only work if your water is supplied by the direct system (see page 69).

Knocking, rattling and water hammer

This can be caused by a number of things.

● Usually it is loose pipes. If the pipes are exposed and easily accessible, check that the saddles or clips holding the pipes are secure. Fit more if necessary.

● There could be an airlock in the system (see above).

● There could be a loose nut in the mains water tap (usually the kitchen tap).

● Check the ball float in the cistern. Replace it if necessary.

● Fit a plastic disc (available at DIY stores or ironmongers) designed to prevent water hammer to the end of the ball valve in the storage cistern. This prevents the ball jumping about, which may cause 'hammering' noises in the water pipes.

Blockages

- Never throw tea leaves, coffee grounds, vegetable peelings or grease down the sink. They build up insidiously.

- Dose the drain once a week with boiling water to prevent grease accumulation.

- Try unblocking your kitchen sink by flushing down a handful of washing soda in 500 ml/½ pint hot water. If this does not work, try the plunger. Block off the overflow, then work the plunger. Do not be too over-enthusiastic, or you could pull the sink off the wall.

- To unblock the U-bend, first stand a bucket under the outlet. Unscrew the outlet plug, and wait for water to gush into the bucket. Push a length of flexible curtain wire down the sink outlet (through the plug hole) and wiggle it about vigorously. When this has been cleared, attack from below. Thrust an old bottle brush up through the open U-bend outlet and ream out the length of pipe leading from the outlet to the drain. When the blockage has gone, flush the pipes out with water. Replace the screw plug. Run the tap to check that the blockage has dispersed.

- Before replacing the U-bend plug, grease the thread with petroleum jelly. This will make it easier to shift on future occasions.

- To unblock a lavatory pan, you will need a larger cup plunger. Steel yourself to scoop out what you can of any visible blockage. (Wear rubber gloves.) Work the plunger up and down in short bursts. When the blockage starts to move, help it on its way with water from a bucket. DO NOT PULL THE CHAIN until the blockage has gone. If you can't get rid of it, call your plumber.

- To unblock an outside drain, put on your rubber gloves, remove the grille cover and scrub it with hot water and disinfectant. Hose out the drain hole or sluice with buckets of hot water. Scrape sludge from the walls of the drain with an old knife. Tie an old spoon to a length of cane and use the implement to break up and remove the silt at the bottom of the drain. Hose down again, dose with disinfectant and replace the grille.

- Keep drains free from blockage by dosing monthly with a cup full of washing soda in a jug of water. If you are surrounded by trees, invest in a wire cage drain cover to keep dead leaves out of the drain.

Water filled radiators

- Learn to 'bleed' your hot water filled radiators. Hardware and DIY shops supply radiator keys if you lose yours. Bleeding will get rid of trapped air which will prevent the radiator from doing its job properly.

- Stand an old cup under the radiator inlet while bleeding to catch odd drips and squirts.

- Turn the nut until you hear a slight hiss, followed by a splutter of water. When the hissing stops, tighten the nut again.

Plumbing tool kit

Keep a set of tools to deal with plumbing emergencies:

- Adjustable spanner. Medium size (20 cm) version has has jaws that open up to 2.5 cm. Use on copper pipe compression fittings, nuts and bolts.

— A set of open ended Whitworth spanners. Use to deal with most nuts.

— Pliers. Use for cutting wire, pulling split pins.

— Adjustable grip. Use for removing rusted bolts or parts as it can be clamped in place, giving lots of leverage and leaving you a free hand.

— Blowtorch with butane gas cartridges. Use to sweat copper solder. DO NOT USE ON GAS PIPES.

— Medium sized cup plunger. Use to deal with sink blockages.

ELECTRICITY

Although it is not advisable to undertake large-scale wiring jobs about the home, you should be able to rewire plugs at the very least, understand how your electrical system works and, more importantly, how to make it safe while you make small repairs.

Mains electricity comes into your house through a service cable which passes through a sealed box called the *supply service cut out*. This contains the main fuse and is the property and responsibility of your Electricity Board. From the service cut out, the cable passes through the meter, which measures the flow, to your consumer unit. The meter is also Electricity Board property.

The consumer unit (or fuse box as was) is an oblong, wall-mounted box with a cover over the fuses and an on/off switch. (Sometimes this is mounted next to the unit in a separate box.) This is what you switch off when you want to stop all electrical flow into the house. You *must* switch it off before looking into the consumer unit or undertaking any electrical repairs in the house.

In the consumer unit are a number of fuses or, sometimes

on modern installations, circuit breakers, which protect the various electrical circuits. There is one for each 30 amp circuit (usually 2); one for each 5 amp circuit (lighting, usually 2), one for the 15 amp or 20 amp circuit which serves the immersion heater, and one for the 45-60 amp circuit which supplies the cooker. There may be others, eg for the shower. It is a good idea to label these for your own reference.

If something goes wrong in any of the circuits, the fuse will rupture or the circuit breaker will open, cutting off the supply to that circuit. You then switch off all power, investigate, make the repair/call the electrician, replace the fuse wire or cartridge or reset the breaker (by pressing the button) and switch on again.

You may also have a residual current circuit breaker (RCCB) mounted beside the consumer unit. This acts as a further safety guard, which operates if there is an earthing fault anywhere. If it is tripped, you must switch off the power, and investigate all the circuits as above.

Once inside the house, your supply is carried by cable of various thicknesses. Each cable contains a live wire (insulated in *red* plastic sheathing), by a neutral wire (sheathed in *black*) and an earth wire (uninsulated). Electricity works when a circuit is continuous from the live wire at the consumer unit through the equipment and back through the neutral wire. The red wire is live and conducts the supply, the black wire is the neutral and returns it. Sockets and light fittings are connected to these circuits. When they are switched off, the circuit is broken; when they are switched on, the circuit can be completed and the power flows. A short circuit is the result of uninsulated wires touching each other and completing the circuit spontaneously. The earth wire is included in cable and flex to conduct rogue electricity safely away, rather than electrifying the whole appliance should there be a fault.

The flex used to connect appliances to the system repeats the cable, with a live wire (*brown* sheathing) a neutral wire (*blue*) and an earth (*green and yellow*).

Electrical power is distributed around the house in two ways. Old houses tend to have radial circuits. A separate cable runs out to each socket and each cable has its own fuse. This becomes cumbersome when homes require a large number of sockets.

Modern systems are supplied by ring circuits. These work in a continuous loop, both ends being connected to the consumer unit. This gives more flexibility and capacity for the same size of cable as the power can come from both directions.

Lighting is supplied on the 5 amp circuit. It is either a junction box circuit, in which the cable runs through a set of junction boxes from which come two further cables supplying the ceiling rose and the light switch respectively; or it is a loop-in system, which treats the ceiling roses themselves as junction boxes. Wiring cables run from the ceiling rose to the switch while a flex (which must contain an earth wire if metal fittings are used) feeds the lights.

When to call the electrician

- When your fuses/circuit breakers continue to blow/trip when you cannot trace the fault.

- When the residual current circuit breaker refuses to reset.

- When your wiring is over 25 years old and/or you have round pin sockets instead of square pin or you can see damaged insulation sockets and other wiring damage.

Electrical terms you need to know

Volts measure the force of electricity. In the UK, the standard domestic supply is 240 volts.

Amps measure the quantity of electricity passing through; plugs and conductors are rated in amps to show how much electricity they can safely carry.

Watts measure the amount of electricity an appliance used when it is operating. A Kilowatt is 1000 watts.

Socket recommendation

It is always better to have more than enough sockets, but if you are not certain how many you might need, follow the Electricity Council's recommendations.

Kitchen at least four 13 amp sockets (excluding outlets for fixed appliances such as cookers, dishwashers, fridges, freezers, washing machine, clock).
Living Room 6 sockets (excluding radiant fire sockets).
Dining Room 3 13 amp sockets.
Double Bedroom 4 13 amp sockets.
Single Bedroom 3 13 amp sockets.
Landing 1 13 amp socket (it may be better to make this a double one).
Hall 1 13 amp socket (again, a double one would be better).
Garage 2 sockets (excluding freezer socket). The sockets in the garage should be protected by a residual current device (RCD) because the equipment used from these sockets will probably extend to the garden. Any socket supplying a freezer should preferably be wired separately from any RCD protected wiring.

Running costs

Your meter measures electricity in units, and your Electricity Board charges you by the unit. A unit is 1 kilowatt hour, this is 1000 watts used continuously for one hour. You should therefore be able to make an estimate of your consumption by noting the wattage of your various appliances and how long you use them. For example, a cassette deck (30 watts) can be played non-stop for 33 hours before it consumes one unit.

Below are listed the consumption, in watts and units, of the commonest household appliances. These figures are an average, referring to a family of four in a medium sized house. Obviously there will be slight variations. More information on appliance consumption may be obtained from your Electricity Board who have leaflets on this topic.

Electric Blanket

    Single underblanket   60 watts

        1½ hours per night for 7 nights: less than 1 unit.

    Double underblanket   120 watts

        1½ hours per night for 7 nights: 1½ units.

    Single overblanket   150 watts

        All night for 7 nights: 2 units.

    Double overblanket   150 watts

        All night for 7 nights: 3 units.

Blender   200 watts

    250 1/500 pints of soup: 1 unit.

Coffee Percolator   750 watts

    75 cups of coffee: 1 unit.

Cooker   12000 watts

    1 week's meals for the family: 17 units.

Dishwasher   3000 watts

    1 full load: 2 units.

Fan Heater   3000 watts without thermostat.

    30 minutes heat: 1½ units.

Food processor   120-700 watts

    60 cakes mixed: 1 unit.

Freezer (upright)	300 watts 1-2 units per day.
Fridge/Freezer	100-300 watts 1-2 units per day
Hair dryer	350-800 watts 12 ten minute sessions: 1-2 units.
Iron	1000 watts 2 hours continuous ironing: 1 unit.
Kettle	2000-3000 watts 6 1/12 pints boiling water: 1 unit.
Lamp	60 watts 16 hours light: 1 unit
Microwave Oven	600 watts 2 joints of beef (1.3 kg/3 lb): 1 unit.
Radiator (oil filled)	500 watts 2 hours: 1 unit.
Radiant fire	3000 watts 20 minutes: 1 unit
Refrigerator	100 watts One day: 1 unit.
Shaver	16 watts 1800 shaves: 1 unit.
Shower	7000 watts Quick shower (5 mins) every day for a week: 3-4 units.

Spin dryer	300 watts 5 weekly loads: 1 unit.
Stereo record player	75 watts 8-10 hours: 1 unit.
Tape Recorder	25-75 watts 24 hours: 1 unit.
Tea Maker	500 watts 35 cups of tea: 1 unit.
TV (22 in. colour)	100 watts 6-9 hours viewing: 1 unit.
Toaster	1050-1360 watts 70 slices of toast: 1 unit.
Tumble dryer	2500 watts. 30 mins: 1 unit.
Vacuum cleaner	
Cylinder	500 watts 1½ hours: 1 unit.
Upright	500 watts 2 hours: 1 unit
Washing Machine	
Automatic	2500 watts 1 weekly family wash: 5 units.
Twin Tub	2500 watts 1 weekly family wash: 12 units.
Water Heater	
Instant water heater	3000 watts 12 1/3 gallons hot water: 1 unit.

Immersion heater	3000 watts
	Hot water for one week for family of four: 67 units with correct lagging jacket on the tank.

Safety first

- Never use portable electric appliances in the bathroom.

- Switch off at the mains and remove fuses or circuit breakers before undertaking repair.

- Do not get into bed with the electric underblanket plugged in unless it is specially designed for this kind of use.

- Never handle switches etc. with wet hands.

- Do not buy cheap plugs that do not conform to BS No. 1363 (March 1988).

- Replace cracked or broken plugs immediately.

- Ensure that the plug has the correct fuse.

- If moving plug from one appliance to another, make sure fuse is correct.

- Full size electric cookers must be wired in with their own 45 and 30 amp circuits. Table top cookers can be connected with plugs and sockets.

- Choose electrical items that have been approved by BEAB (see Addresses) *WHICH?* or GH approved. Never buy secondhand goods.

- Never wind flex around the iron when it is still hot.

- Never pull plugs out by the flex.

- Never repair frayed electric flexes with insulating tape. Replace the entire flex.

- Never throw away instruction leaflets or service information about electrical appliances. Store them in a plastic wallet file in a handy place.

- When storing appliance flexes together, tag each one by snapping on plastic tags (the kind that come on bread) or sticking plaster and write the name on each tag with a felt tip.

- Unplug sockets not in use at night after you have switched them off.

- Switch off and unplug steam irons before filling or refilling.

- Make sure flex from kettles etc. does not trail across hot plates or drape over the edges of working surfaces.

- Do not leave soft toys near or under lamps.

- Never run an electrical appliance from a light socket.

- Never undertake any electrical repair work without switching off at the mains.

- Check that sockets are 'dead' by plugging in a previously working table lamp. (If it lights up when you switch on, switch off and go back to the mains and check the current.)

- If you use flexed appliances (DIY tools etc.) a lot, consider using an RCD adapter. (RCD means residual current device.) This plugs into the socket, then the appliance plugs into the adapter. This cuts off the current automatically if it detects a leakage of electricity to earth. You can have the whole wiring system protected in this way but may be quite expensive and inconvenient.

General hints

- Invest in a buzzplug for your freezer (or any other appliance which has to stay on permanently). This has a built in alarm which goes off if the fuse blows or the power goes off.

- Do not obstruct the ventilation of fridges or freezers.

- Never prise toast from the toaster with a metal knife, fork or spoon. *Switch it off.* Turn the toaster upside down and coax the toast out with a wooden spoon or a spatula.

- Keep torches, batteries, matches, candles, fuse wire and cartridge fuses near the meter. Check the torch batteries regularly.

- To prevent small children sticking things into sockets, use plastic shield plugs or three pinned night light plugs which shine in the dark. Modern sockets have gates which come down automatically when plugs are removed, but it is better to be safe than sorry.

- Use 3 pin plug night-lights in dark corners or to light the route to the lavatory at night.

- If your house is more than 25 years old, have the wiring checked.

- Have all electrical appliances serviced as recommended by their manufacturers. The cost of this may be included in the price or guarantee.

- Have your wiring checked every 5-10 years.

Electric blankets

- If you are using an electric blanket on bunk beds, tape the flex to keep it out of the way of the lower bunk.

- Never use an electric overblanket as an under-blanket.

- Switch off underblankets before getting into bed.

- Electric blankets should have a plug fitted with a 3 amp fuse.

- When choosing a blanket, look for BS 3456 and BEAB approval, and make sure it has overheat protection.

- Always tie underblankets to the mattress.

- Don't store with camphor.

- Don't dry clean.

- Don't fold the blanket, particularly while switched on.

- Don't use pins or needles on it.

- Don't tuck it in.

- Don't use for children.

- Have it serviced every year.

- Do not use a hot water bottle at the same time as an electric blanket.

Adaptors

- Remember that adaptors are temporary measures. If you need them regularly, you do not have enough sockets.

- Adaptors must contain their own cartridge fuse (usually 13 amp).

- What you plug into an adaptor must not exceed the capacity of its fuse.

- Don't let the adaptor sit loosely in the socket, or the

plugs work loose in the adaptor. If the contacts don't meet, the adaptor will overheat.

- If you live in rented accommodation, or where extra sockets are impossible, invest in a portable spur unit. This will provide 4 or 5 sockets and a pilot light to indicate that it is live. You can move this from room to room, and it avoids lots of trailing flex.

Lighting

- Low wattage bulbs often provide a pleasanter atmosphere (don't use them for working areas) and are cheaper to run.

- Consider fluorescent lamps in work areas, kitchens and bathrooms. The light is better and it costs 50 per cent less than conventional bulbs.

- Fit dimmer switches in living and sleeping areas. The saving in electricity will soon cover your initial outlay.

- Clean light bulbs give better light. Switch off the light, remove the light bulb. Clean it with cotton wool moistened with methylated spirit.

- Do not exceed wattage recommendations given on lamp shades. Too powerful a bulb is a fire hazard.

Economy measures

- Turn thermostat or heating controls down one degree. You will not notice any appreciable change in temperature, but you could cut heating costs by 10 per cent over the quarter.

- Make the most of Economy 7 which is available for 7 hours at night, or white meter electricity, usually from midnight to 7 am. It is half the standard rate.

- Keep your curtains drawn (or the blinds down) as soon as it is dark. This stops heat escaping. Consider lining your curtains with insulating fabric.

- Shower rather than bath. It costs less.

- Do not open the fridge and freezer doors unnecessarily.

- Invest in time switches so that you can run immersion heaters, washing machines, tumble dryers and dishwashers on cheaper power at night. Some models of washing machines and tumble dryers are supplied with a 'delay' control. It is worth shopping around.

NB Never fit plug-in timers to portable heaters or radiant fires. If they switch on while unattended they could start a fire.

- Always fill the freezer, or keep it at least ¾ full (bulk buy bread if necessary). Never put hot food in – let it cool first.

- Defrost refrigerators and freezers regularly according to manufacturers' instructions. An iced-up freezer or refrigerator costs more to run.

- Always use your washing machine and tumble dryer to capacity. Many models now come with a half-load facility, but before you use it check with the manufacturers' instructions. (If you wash delicate fabrics on a half load they will come out of the machine crumpled.)

- Check that your loft insulation is the recommended depth or thickness. In most homes, this means 100 mm/4 in. insulation in the roofspace. Lagging on the hot water tank should be 80 m/3 in. thick.

- When cooking, match pan and hob ring size.

- Boil water in an electric kettle rather than on a ring.

Electric tools

You do not have to be a DIY expert to do small electrical repairs. Below are listed the basic tools that every home should have. Keep them separate from general DIY kit.

— Screwdrivers with insulated plastic handles.

— Pliers with insulated handles and cutting edges.

— Wire strippers.

— Insulated (rubber clad) torch.

— Selection of fuses (and fuse wire).

— Main tester (this is a screwdriver with an insulated handle with a neon bulb which lights up when the screwdriver blade touches a live terminal).

Wiring a plug

Anyone can learn to do this. You need a screwdriver and wire strippers (or a sharp knife or scissors).

- Unscrew plug cover. Remove one flex clamp screw and loosen the other.

- Lever out the fuse. (Get replacement ready if necessary.) Loosen terminal screws. Most plugs have three terminals: live, earth and neutral.

- Lay the flex in the plug, cutting the three wires to reach about 13 mm/½ in. beyond each terminal. The green and yellow wire goes to the earth terminal (marked E); the blue wire goes to neutral (marked N); the brown wire goes to the live terminal (marked L).

- Strip away enough insulation on each wire to expose about 6 mm/¼ in. copper wire to fit into screwhole terminals terminals mm/¼ in. copper wire to fit into screwhole terminals (where wire goes through terminal pillars) or 13 mm/½ in. for clamp terminals (in which the wire winds round the terminal pillars). Twist the strands of copper wire together before placing in the terminal.

- Fasten the clamp firmly over the flex. Fit each wire into its correct terminal hole and tighten each screw. (If dealing with clamp terminals, wrap wire clockwise around) terminals before tightening screws.)

- Double check that the wires are connected correctly; that there are no stray whiskers of copper wire; that the flex clamp is on the outer sheath of the cable, not on the wires; and that all the screws are tight.

- Refit (or replace) the correct fuse and replace plug cover.

- If the terminal wires are small, try folding them over first before putting them into the terminal holes.

- If you are changing plugs from a different appliance, check that the fuse is the correct size.

- Some appliances are fitted with a non-rewirable plug. Change the fuses on this kind of plug by prising out the fuseholder (between the three pins) with a screwdriver. Replace the fuse, refit the fuseholder.

- Remove and properly dispose of faulty moulded on plugs which have been cut off appliances. Do not leave them around where children may find them. They may be plugged into sockets and produce live wires at the cut-off point.

Reading the meter

- Always read your own electricity meter. More and more Electricity Boards are sending out estimated bills. As these are always based on previous quarters, they may not always be correct. Estimated readings are always marked with an E. There is a space on the back of your electricity bill where you can fill in your own reading.

- If your meter is digital, read off the numbers; to work out your exact consumption, subtract the previous reading from the latest one.

- If your meter is an economy 7 or white meter, there are two rows of figures, one for day and one for night units.

- If you have a dial meter, the reading is rather more complicated. Always write down the number the pointer has just *passed*, not the one it is approaching; if the pointer is directly over a figure, and the next reading is on 9, the previous figure is reduced by one.

- Work out a yearly budget by monitoring your meter once a month. Check against past consumption in the home, taking into account new equipment or extra rooms being used due to sickness etc.

Fuses

- Always use the correct fuses. Too high a rating defeats the object of a fuse (safety) and too low will cause unnecessary failures. Follow this guide:

  — 3 amp (red) fuses for appliances up to 720 watts. (Note that some appliances require 13 amp because of motor starting surges.)

— 13 amp (brown) fuses for appliances from 720-3,000 watts.

TVs, cookers and shower units are exceptions. TVs take 5 or 13 amp fuses. Cooker circuits use prewired 45 amp fuses and shower units have 30 or 45 amp fuses.

- Check fuses with the help of a metal cased torch. Unscrew the torch bottom; place one end of the fuse on the battery bottom and the other end on the torch casing. Switch the torch on. If the torch bulb does not light up, the fuse has blown. (Make sure the torch is working first.)

- If fuses continue to blow do *not* fit a larger one. Have the appliance checked, or call in professional help to examine the socket and/or the whole system.

- Label the circuits in your consumer unit so you can easily identify which has blown.

Power failure

During a power failure, take the following precautions to prevent disaster when the power returns:

- Switch off all appliances such as irons, heaters and machinery in case the power returns while you are away.

- Keep a torch, spare batteries, candles and matches in an accessible place easy to find in the dark. Make sure all the family knows where these are kept. Keep a duplicate set on a shelf near the electricity meter.

- If the power is out for longer than an hour, wrap heated tropical fish aquaria in blankets.

GAS

The gas supply comes into your house via a mains pipe and is connected to the meter. There is a main gas tap, which looks like a lever, fitted at the point of entry. This is what you should switch off (pull it down) if there are any problems. You should not undertake any gas repairs yourself. However, you can learn your way about the system and learn how to cut off the supply and maintain your gas appliances in good order.

General tips

- Have all unused gas pipes capped off and plugged, or removed.

- Make a note of your Gas Board's emergency number and keep it by the telephone with your other emergency numbers.

- To turn off the main gas tap, pull the lever down so that the notched line across the tap spindle is horizontal.

- Before switching off, turn out all gas taps and pilot lights.

- To turn it back on again, first check that all gas taps are off. Then pull the lever upright so that the notched mark on the spindle is vertical. Then light all pilot lights.

- Test the gas tap routinely. If it is stiff DO NOT FORCE IT. Call the Gas Board, who will come and deal with it.

- If the tap is in an inaccessible position, have it moved. Contact the Gas Board.

- If you go away for some time, it is a good idea to turn the gas supply off as shown.

- Have all gas appliances serviced every two years. Central heating, water heaters and fires should be serviced at least once a year.

- Keep airvents clear. Do not succumb to the temptation of blocking up every orifice and cranny in a room to keep warm. Unless gas fires and other appliances have sufficient air, they will become very dangerous, and may begin to produce carbon monoxide, which is poisonous.

- Have chimneys swept thoroughly if you intend to fit a gas fire in an old coal fireplace. A blocked chimney will prevent gas fumes escaping.

- Check fires and heaters for telltale signs of trouble: sooty deposits and discolourations and yellow or orange coloured flames. Call the gas board or an accredited gas engineer immediately.

- Avoid second hand gas appliances. They account for 50 per cent of the reported gas accidents with faulty applicances.

- Report gas leaks immediately, even if they are not in your house.

Gas water heaters

- Open the bathroom window while running hot water into the bath.

- Turn the water off before getting into the bath, and do not run more hot water into the bath.

- Do not run instant water heaters for longer than 5 minutes continuously. They are not designed for this purpose.

- Do not shower or wash your hair directly under the tap of a bathroom water heater.

Running costs

Gas is charged by the therm, which is 100,000 British Thermal Units (BTU). A BTU is the amount of heat needed to raise 1 lb weight of water (or 280 l) 1 degree Fahrenheit above 32° (or from 10°C to 100°C). What can you do with a therm?

One therm will:

- Boil 80 l/160 pints of water in the kettle

- Cook 5 days worth of family meals

- Provide hot water for 5 baths or 15 showers

- Run a small fridge for 7 days

- Run a gas fire for about 8 hours

- Provide 250 l/63 gallons of hot water at 63°C/140°F.

Gas leak

If you suspect a gas leak do the following:

- Put out cigarettes/cigars/pipes instantly.

- Do not use matches or naked flames.

- Open all windows and doors.

- Do not use any electrical machines or switch on lights; not even doorbells. A slight spark could trigger an explosion.

- Check all gas taps and pilots and turn them off.

- Turn off the supply at the meter.

- Keep off all gas taps while the supply is off in case it returns unexpectedly.

- Call the Gas Board.

HEATING AND INSULATION

Most central heating requires little maintenance by the householder. Insulation and draught proofing are relevant whatever sort of heating system (gas, oil-fired, electric, solid fuel) you have. Remember that over zealous insulation can provide just as many problems (condensation, rot etc) as no insulation at all.

General heating tips

- Keep gas boilers free of dust and dirt to maintain a good flow of air.

- Have central heating boilers serviced once a year.

- Have chimneys swept regularly.

- Avoid radiant electrical fires/heaters in small rooms. There must be at least 1 m/3 feet from the heater to furniture to avoid scorching and possibly fire.

- Do not hang curtains above convector or storage heaters.

- Do not use convector heaters to dry clothes.

- Never use time switches on radiant electrical heaters.

Insulation and draught proofing

- In most homes, heat losses can be reduced by almost 20 per cent if you install 100 mm/4 in. thick insulation in the roof space.

- Installing your own roof space insulation is simple. Here are the rules:

  — Do the work on a cool day.

  — Calculate the loft area roughly; do not worry about small protrusions.

- Wear gloves, all-in-one overalls, goggles and a mask if you are installing glass fibre blanket insulation.

- Wear dust masks if pouring 'loose-lay' insulation (granules, mica or vermiculite).

• NEVER put insulation underneath the cold water tank. It will get too cold unless warmth from the room below can get to it.

• Eschew over-enthusiasm; it is not necessary to insulate the sloping walls of the roof; if you do, you will encourage condensation.

• Don't forget to lag pipes in garages or outhouses.

• Hot water cylinders not already lagged should have a jacket of insulation at least 80 mm/3 in. thick. This cuts down heat loss by almost 33 per cent.

• Fit draught excluder strips round doors and windows. This can save up to 1000 units (1 kWh) in the colder months. Draughts account for almost 10 per cent of heat loss.

• Choose the right strip for the job when draught proofing doors. The foam strip is best for doors opening onto hard floors; brush strips are best for doors opening onto carpets.

• Check that the door is warp-free before fitting metal insulation strips.

• Fit brush-style insulation strips to letterboxes so that letters can get through.

• Fit escutcheon plates to keyholes if possible.

• Double glazing is very expensive, and you may not need it if you insulate the rest of the house properly.

If you have large expanses of glass to cover, you can use the clear plastic film that shrinks onto the window when 'blown dry' with a hairdryer on a low setting. If this produces considerable heat saving, then consider investigating double glazing.

- Old wooden floors can be draughty. Block up any holes or gaps.

- If the wind whistles through the gap between floor and skirting board, fit quadrant (quarter round) moulding or beading.

- Do *not* seal off air bricks. Dry rot (see page 66) thrives in warm dry air, so underfloor air circulation is essential.

- Do not insulate everything in sight! Condensation caused by over-zealous insulation can cause as much of a problem as draughts and heat loss.

- Radiators throw one quarter of their heat backwards, that is, out of the house. You can redirect this heat inwards by lining the wall behind it with kitchen foil.

- If you have not already stuck insulation foil on the wall before the radiators have been installed, it is possible to put it up afterwards. Switch the radiator off first. Paste one side of the foil with wallpaper paste. Drop it down behind the radiator. To stick it on the wall, use a sponge-head mop attached to a cane, or pad a wire coat-hanger with foam rubber and attach that by the handle to the cane. You can buy radiator rollers specially designed for the job.

FIREPLACES AND CHIMNEYS

- Sweep chimneys regularly to clear birds' nests, soot blockage etc. If you discover that bricks or cement dating from the chimney's building are blocking the way, you will have to have the chimney rebuilt.

- If you suspect that your chimney is on fire, call the fire brigade immediately. Move the hearth-rug and any other flammable material away from the danger zone.

- If your fire smokes, and the chimney and fuel are sound, the fireplace opening may be too high or too large. As a rough rule, the dimensions of the fireplace should be about 10 times larger than those of the flue (6 times if the fire is on the second floor or in a bungalow.) If the dimensions do not tally, you will need expert help. Contact the Solid Fuel Advisory Service (see Addresses).

6

General hints

Below are some ingenious tips designed to make life a little easier. The subjects are arranged alphabetically.

Adhesive Tape

- Place a small button at the end of the roll to make the end easier to find.

- If a roll of adhesive tape has become 'gummed up', steam it for a couple of seconds.

Aluminium

- Polish aluminium with dry table salt. (This is not recommended on anodised or mirror finish aluminium.)
  Aluminium saucepans (see SAUCEPANS).

Batteries

- Do not use new batteries with old ones. The new ones try to recharge the old and lose some of their own potency.

Blankets

Wool (see page 35).
Electric (see page 89).

Breadbins

- Prevent mildew developing by occasionally wiping out the breadbin with a clean cloth wrung out in a vinegar and water solution (15 ml/2 tbsp water to 450 ml/1 pint water).

Bath Mats

- Always hang bath mats on a rail to dry when not in use.

- Use mild bleach solution to get rid of mould on non-slip bath mats.

Bath Towels

- Cut up old bath towels to make a patchwork beach towel.

Brooms and Mops

- Prevent damage to skirting boards by nailing a strip of draught excluder round the broom head.

- Store brooms hanging up (head uppermost if it's possible).

- Rinse floor mops out with a warm, mild disinfectant solution to kill off bacteria. Hang them out to dry in a well-ventilated area.

- Store PVA sponge mops with their heads in a polythene bag.

- Don't use bleach with cellulose mops. They will disintegrate.

Cakes and Biscuits

- Cake will remain moist if you include a slice of bread (remove when dried out) or an eating apple in the tin.

- Biscuits will stay crisp if you keep some sugar cubes in the tin with them.

Candles

- Candles will last longer if they are stored in the freezer for a few hours before they are used.

- Mend broken candles by softening the lower end with boiling water. Ram the top on and hold it in place until it has set.

- Straighten bent candles by placing them in a polythene bag and hold it under the hot water tap. When the candles have softened, roll them gently on a flat surface to straighten them.

Candlesticks

- To remove wax from candlesticks first chip off as much as possible. Then play a hairdryer (on low heat) over the rest of the wax until it melts and can be washed off in warm soapy water.

Cast Iron

- Clean the outside of cast iron utensils with a proprietary oven cleaner. Rinse thoroughly.

- Wipe the inside of cast iron pots and pans with corn oil before putting them away, to prevent rusting.

Chopping Boards

- To get rid of strong smells, such as garlic, smear the board with a paste of bicarbonate of soda and water. Leave for a few minutes, scrub thoroughly and rinse in cold water. Store upright.

- Clean used pastry boards by sprinkling with salt and rubbing with the palm of your hand. Wash, rinse well in cold water and stand to dry.

Corkscrew

- If you have mislaid your corkscrew, improvise. Insert a long screw into the cork, tie a length of string to its head and pull.

Cups

- Remove stains from Melamine cups with a little toothpaste. For stubborn stains, try a little washing powder on a damp cloth. Rinse well.

Curtains (see also page 35)

- Old net curtains can come in useful. They make excellent bath cleaners, as they are mildly abrasive but do not scratch. They are also useful as fly screens over pet cages.

Decanters

- To clean out decanters use a mixture of warm water and vinegar (equal parts) and half a cup of clean sand (playsand). Shake hard and leave to stand.

- Use a Steradent tablet, or other foaming false teeth cleaner. Dissolve according to instructions. Leave overnight. Rinse well.

- If stopper gets stuck, apply a drop or two of warmed cooking oil around the edge. Leave in a warm place. Strike stopper gently with a wooden spoon handle on the side, then ease it out.

Drawers

- Save leftover wallpaper to line drawers, but do not use ready-pasted vinyl in food cupboards.

- Rub the stub of a candle or a bar of soap along drawer runners to prevent sticking.

Earthenware

- Do not wash unglazed earthenware in detergent or soap. Clean it in a solution of hot water and salt or vinegar.

Foil

- You can use kitchen foil more than once. Soak used piece in hot detergent mixture, brush gently, rinse and smooth out.

- If you don't have a foil dispenser, store foil rolls on rods mounted across the width of a drawer about 2.5 cm/1 in. from the top.

Fridges/Freezers

- Leave door (or lid of chest freezer) open when you have switched off to prevent mould.

- Brush glycerine on the underside of ice cube trays after defrosting. They will not stick to the shelf next time you need them.

- Wipe out fridges with a solution of 10-15 ml/2-3 tsp bicarbonate of soda in 1 l/1¾ pints water to get rid of smells.

- To absorb smells, place a tray of loose charcoal (for barbecues) or a saucer of clean cat litter. This is particularly useful when you go away for a long weekend or a holiday.

Frying Pans

- Rub salt into new or clean frying pans with paper. This will promote a non-stick effect. (Of course, this is not suitable for 'non-stick' pans.)

- Never wash omelette pans. Rub them out with a good wad of kitchen paper or crumpled newspaper as soon as they are cool enough to touch.

- Never leave non-stick pans over a heat source with nothing in them. The coating will deteriorate.

Furniture

- There are several remedies for white marks on wooden furniture:

    — camphorated oil

    — metal polish

    — cut half of a Brazil nut

    all these should be rubbed briskly over the area in the direction of the grain, using a soft cloth for the oil and polish. (Valuable and antique furniture should be professionally treated.)

- Remove the build-up of old polish with a chamois leather well wrung out in a solution of 1:8 parts vinegar and warm water. Dry with a soft cloth.

- Hide scratches by filling them with similar coloured wax crayon or shoe polish. Leave for a while then buff well.

- To remove slight dents, lay damp cotton wool over the dent for 2 to 3 hours. The wood below will swell up.

- If you own antique furniture, keep the ambient temperature at 18°C/65°F, and counteract too much drying out by using humidifiers or shallow bowls of water.

- Cure a blister in veneer by cutting it through with a sharp knife. Lay damp cotton wool on top of the cut blister to soften the veneer. Work PVA glue under the blister. Flatten the veneer, lay piece of tissue or brown paper over it and clamp or weight it down until the glue is dry.

- Rub down cigarette burns on wood with fine steel wool. Rub linseed oil in and leave overnight. Polish.

Hairbrushes

- Polish real tortoiseshell backed brushes with furniture cream on a soft cloth.

- Never wet the backs of ivory-backed brushes while cleaning the bristles. Clean the ivory parts with cotton wool dampened with white spirit. (Do not use this on valuable ivory.)

- After washing genuine bristle brushes, rinse the bristles in cold water to stiffen them.

Handbags (Canvas)

- Spray canvas bags with fabric guard as soon as you can after buying.

- Clean canvas bags with a damp cloth moistened with clear liquid bath cleaner. Rinse with a wet cloth and leave to dry naturally. Spray with fabric guard to prevent re-soiling.

Handbags (Leather)

- Only use a neutral shoe polish on leather bags. Coloured polish may rub off on your clothes.

Hot Water Bottles

- Add a few drops of glycerine to the water bottle when using a new hot water bottle for the first time. This will help keep the rubber supple.

Jars

- Some ways to loosen screwtop jars:

  — Invert jar and tap metal top at an angle.

  — Heat the lid under running hot tap.

- Wind rubber bands around lid rim to give yourself a better grip.

- Wear rubber gloves to do the job.

- Make jars into flour dredgers or water sprinklers by punching small holes with a bradawl into the lid.

- Save pretty jars to use for your own home-made chutneys, mincemeat and marmalade.

Juice Cartons

- Save juice cartons. Open the top up fully and keep the carton by the kitchen sink. It makes a useful, leakproof receptacle for tea bags, coffee grounds etc. Broken glass can be safely packed into juice cartons before being thrown away, to prevent dustbin liners being torn open.

Kettle

- Descale furred kettles by boiling equal quantities of vinegar and water. Allow to cool off overnight. Clean out the following day.

- Alternatively, use a solution of citric acid crystals (10 ml/2 tsp citric acid crystals to 500 ml/1 pint warm water). Rinse well before using. Check with manufacturer's instructions first if your kettle is new.

- Don't put more water in the kettle than you need, but always cover the element of an electric kettle.

- Store boiled water that you don't need in a vacuum flask for use later that day.

Keys

- Stick a square of fluorescent tape or small round sticker onto your key to make it easier to find in your handbag at night.

Knives

- Do not immerse bone handles of knives in water.

- Remove stains from bone handles with salt on a damp cloth.

- Rub carbon steel knife blades with a wet cork dipped in scouring powder (or mildly abrasive scouring pad). Rinse immediately and dry. Never put carbon steel blade knives in the dishwasher.

- As a temporary measure you can sharpen knives by drawing the blade across the side of a bottle.

- If you use a magnetic knife rack, hang the knives point uppermost. Then if they fall off, they will stand less chance of being blunted (or kebabing anyone's foot).

- Rub the cut surface of a lemon on yellowing ivory knife handles.

- Sharpen carbon steel bladed knives on an oilstone.

Loofah

- Cut up old or festering loofahs and use the offcuts for cleaning paintwork etc. Loofah pads will not scratch non-stick pans.

Mattresses

- Do not use a vacuum cleaner on a spring interior mattress, it will dislodge the filling. Use a stiff brush and dustpan instead.

- Turn over or swing round spring interior mattresses from head to foot once a week when new, for a month or so to help the filling settle. After that, turn it quarterly.

Microwaves

- To clean inside a microwave, slice up a lemon and put the slices in an uncovered dish of water. Bring to the boil for five minutes. Remove the dish then wipe out oven.

- Use your microwave for things other than cooking. Most manufacturers supply instructions on how to dry herbs, flowers and grasses. They can also be used to sterilise baby's bottles (instructions usually given with bottle), dishtowels, and jamjars for home preserves.

Mirrors

- Prevent condensation on bathroom mirrors by rubbing over with a little neat washing-up liquid on a soft cloth. Buff with a dry cloth afterwards.

- Remove hairspray from mirrors with a soft cloth moistened with methylated spirit. Finish with proprietary window cleaner.

Oven Gloves

- Sew small magnets into your oven gloves or gauntlets so you can attach them to the side of the cooker.

Photographic Film

- Keep undeveloped and unexposed film in its packaging in the fridge. This will prevent deterioration of the chemicals on the film.

Pianos

- Clean real ivory piano keys with a little toothpaste on a wrung-out damp cloth. Wipe off with milk and polish with a soft cloth. Do not allow liquid to trickle between keys.

- Remove yellowing from ivory keys by rubbing them gently with the cut surface of a fresh lemon.

NB Antique or expensive pianos should be treated by a professional.

Rubber Gloves

- To make rubber gloves last longer, turn them inside out and stick a strip of waterproof sticking plaster across each fingertip. This is especially useful if you have long nails.

- Keep rubber gloves dry and tidy by pegging them together and hanging them (by the peg) on a hook near the sink.

Saucepans

- To clean stained aluminium saucepans, simmer an apple peel or rhubarb in water in the offending pan.

- When washing aluminium pans, add 15 ml/1 tbsp borax to the washing up water to help clean them.

- Remove dents from saucepans by placing the pan on a wooden block and bashing the dents with a hammer with its head wrapped in a soft cloth.

Scales

- Don't stand scales next to the bath or basin. Water could damage the mechanism.

- Don't use abrasive cleaner or chemicals to clean your scales.

- Have scales mechanically checked by professionals (consult retailer or manufacturer).

Shampoo

- Get the most out of shampoo (or bubble bath) bottles by swilling them out with warm water.

Shoes

- Dry out wet shoes (or boots) by stuffing crumpled newspapers in them. This helps them keep their shape.

- Clean shoebrushes by standing the brush, bristles downwards, in a saucer of white spirit to dissolve the polish. Wash in mild detergent and rinse. Stand the brush on its side to dry.

Silver

- To cure black spots, immerse silver in a hot, strong salt solution. Rinse dry and treat with your normal silver polish.

- To clean silver and silver plate cutlery, lay a strip of silver foil 10 cm/4 in. wide across the bottom of a plastic washing-up bowl. Lay the silver on top of it. Add a handful of washing soda, then cover with hot water. When the subsequent bubbling stops, remove the silver and rinse it. Buff up with a soft cloth.

NB Do not treat silver utensils this way if the silver is wearing thin.

Smells

- A burning candle neutralises and dispels cigarette smoke.

- To remove the smell of fish from silver, add 5 ml/1 tsp mustard powder to the washing-up water.

- To remove the smell of fish from china add 5 ml/1 tsp vinegar to the washing-up water.

- Dispel unpleasant bathroom/lavatory smells by lighting a match, holding it upright and letting it burn down for 5 seconds before putting out.

- A cut onion will dispel unpleasant paint smells.

Soap

- Store soap in a warm dry place such as the airing cupboard. The soap will harden, making it last longer.

- Make up soap jelly with leftover soap. Grate about 250 g/½ lb into a bowl and cover with 500 ml/1 pint boiling water and 5 ml/1 tsp borax. Stir until the soap dissolves, pour into a jar and leave until cold. Use the soap jelly as you would the commercially produced 'soft-soap' cleansers.

- Use soap remnants to make a soap sponge for childrens' bathtime. Make a foam rubber 'envelope', leaving a small opening. Put in the soap pieces and oversew the opening, or tuck the flap in.

Sponge

- Soak a slimy sponge in vinegared water (15 ml/1 tbsp vinegar to 500 ml/1 pint water). When the slime has diminished, wash the sponge thoroughly, finally wringing out in warm water.

Steel Wool

- Wrap soap-filled steel wool pads in tinfoil to prevent rust.

- Store steel wool in a jar of soapy water ready for use.

Sticky Labels

- Remove the remnants of sticky labels with methylated spirit, white spirit or cooking oil on kitchen paper. Make a piece of Blu-tak (or similar product) into a ball and rub it over recalcitrant adhesive.

Storage

- Store trays and chopping boards vertically. If you have no ready made space, create some in a cupboard. Use plywood sheets cut to size as dividers. Hold them in place at top and bottom with quadrant beading (available in DIY stores).

- Store sharp objects (skewers, larding needles etc.) safely by sticking corks onto their pointed ends.

- Store your LPs at eye height.

- Store magazines flat if you want to keep them for long term reference.

- Store plates in a cupboard by stacking in a draining board rack/drainer. This keeps them safe and easily accessible.

Suede

- Matted suede can be touched up by rubbing gently with an emery board. Use a suede brush to raise the nap.

Suitcases

- Put a few sugar cubes in your suitcase before storing for the winter. This will prevent mustiness.

- Fasten a wide strip of bright coloured sticky tape across the top of your suitcase to make it easy to spot on a luggage carousel.

Table Mats

- Store table mats on a clipboard hung on a hook in your cupboard. This keeps the mats flat and together in their sets.

Taps

- Remove hard water stains around taps with lemon juice or a salt and vinegar mixture. Leave for five minutes. Rinse thoroughly.

- Clean taps marked with water with a damp cloth dipped in a salt and vinegar paste or dry bicarbonate of soda. Polish with a dry cloth.

Teapots

- To prevent musty smells in your best silver or metal teapot keep a few sugar lumps wrapped in muslin inside.

- Clean silver teapots (and jugs) by putting a handful of milk bottle tops and 15 ml/1 tbsp washing soda inside. Fill with boiling water. Rinse out well. Drain. Dry thoroughly.

  NEVER USE WASHING SODA ON CHROME OR CHROMIUM PLATE OR ALUMINIUM.

- To clean out the teapot spout, pack it with damp salt. Leave overnight. Wash thoroughly with boiling water.

Tea Towels

- Rinse tea and glass cloths in a weak starch solution after washing then you won't get fluff on china and glass.

Tights and Stockings

- Don't be too eager to throw away old tights or stockings. They have many uses (see pages 27, 57, 121).

- Old tights cut up and stuffed into a cotton bag make an excellent polishing pad.

Toothbrushes

- Do not throw old toothbrushes away. There are many uses for them (see page 16, 40, 48).

- Check your toothbrush for wear once a week. Hold it up in front of you, with the back facing you. If you can see the bristles protruding on each side, your toothbrush is no longer helping your teeth. Save it for fiddly cleaning jobs around the house.

Toys

- Test folding toys for safety by placing a pencil in places where little fingers might go. Then see what happens to it when you fold the toy.

- When looking for toys, check for the relevant British Standard number (BS No. 566S). In March 1989 the British Toy and Hobby Manufacturers Association introduced the Lion Mark, a seal of approval featuring a jolly lion logo.

Umbrella Stands

- Cut a piece of foam plastic to fit the base of your stand. This will soak up drips from your umbrellas. Wring it out as necessary.

Vacuum Cleaners

- Invest in an extension lead (a coiled one) for your vacuum to save changing sockets.

- Don't be tempted to false economy by reusing disposable vacuum cleaner bags. The vacuum functions because they are porous. Residual dust builds up, then the vacuum works less efficiently.

Vacuum Flasks

- Freshen up flasks by filling with a solution of 10 ml/ 2 tsp bicarbonate of soda in a flask full of nearly boiling water. Leave overnight. Wash, and rinse out several items.

- Keep a few sugar lumps in a dry flask to keep it fresh when not in use. Leave the stopper resting loosely on the top so air can get in.

- Clean out coffee or tea stains by crushing eggshells and placing them inside with a little hot water. Shake hard. Rinse out with hot water.

Wellington Boots

- Keep children's wellingtons together with a peg. Wooden ones can have your child's name felt-tipped on; younger children will recognize 'their' coloured plastic peg.

- Dry the inside of wet wellingtons with a hairdryer (on a low setting).

7

Flora and fauna

Plants and pets are delightful, but bring their own problems with them. There are many specialist books which deal with animal and indoor plant care but below are a selection of common sense tips which may increase your enjoyment of your animal and vegetable possessions.

GENERAL PLANT TIPS

- Plants need a cool, even temperature. Keep away from draughts and direct heat (including the top of the TV set).

- Don't put plants on top of the radiator or any other heater.

- Don't leave plants in front of the window unless it is curtained or double glazed. Never leave plants behind drawn curtains at night. They could be damaged by the cold atmosphere.

- Store bulbs packed into old tights or stockings. Then you can hang them up so that air can circulate around them.

- Moisten bulb fibre by punching holes in the bag it comes in and immersing this in a bucket of water until the fibre is soaked. Squeeze it almost dry in your fingers before using.

- Keep greenfly away from houseplants by burying a clove of garlic in the soil. Standing the pot on a mirror is supposed to discourage greenfly.

- If you have whitefly in your conservatory, plant a hanging basket with a species of tobacco plant (*Nicotiana*). All the whitefly will home in on this 'trap' and you can then empty out the basket contents onto the fire.

- Herbs do very well in hanging baskets if you are short of space.

- When watering from the top, stop when water runs out from the bottom of the pot. Allow them to stand in the water for 10-15 minutes, then throw excess water away.

- To keep humidity constant, stand your pot inside a larger one and pack the gap with peat. Keep the peat moist.

- Alternatively, rest the pot on a saucer of small pebbles in water. Don't let the water touch the pot.

- Make a holiday greenhouse for your plants when you are away. Fill the bath with 15 cm/6 in. of water. Put the plants in, raised above the water level on buckets or trays. Make a plastic tent over them by taping one end of a sheet of polythene to the wall and draping the rest over the side of the bath. You can do the same with a flat-bottomed sink if it is near a suitable wall.

- To test for watering, press the soil with a piece of newspaper. If the paper becomes damp, the plant is wet enough.

- Water parched plants by plunging them into buckets so that the rim of the plant pot is submerged. Bubbles will appear if the soil is very dried out. Take the plants out of the buckets when the bubbling stops.

- If plants have been overwatered, stand the pot on several thicknesses of newspaper to drain off excess.

- For holiday watering, stand your plants around a bucket of water. Tie a pebble onto one end of a long wick (plain unwaxed string will do). Wedge the other end into the plant compost. Do this for each plant. The water will syphon along the wick from the bucket. (Make sure it is functioning before you leave.)

- To water tender plants, keep your filled watering can in a sunny spot.

- Use an old washing-up liquid bottle (completely cleaned out) as a watering can. The nozzle will allow you to direct the water where you want it.

- Turn plants regularly to prevent lop-sided growth.

- Save lolly sticks to use as markers for seedlings.

- Inverted jars make excellent mini-cloches for seedlings. Sow 3 under each pot and pinch out the weakest after germination.

- Do not use oil or detergent on leaves to make them shiny. Water is best.

- When repotting, clean soil from leaves with a pastry brush. Do not let the leaves get wet.

- Do not throw out broken terracotta pots. Break them up and use for drainage at the bottom of new pots.

- Do not use garden soil for indoor plants. You will import unwanted bacteria, which will multiply in the warmth of the house.

- Scrub out old clay pots before using to eliminate possible infection.

- If you are standing plant pots in baskets, put a foil dish or layer of foil with the edges turned up at the bottom first, to prevent the basket becoming soggy.

- Mix coffee and tea grounds into the soil if you are growing ferns.

Bottle gardens

- When filling/recharging bottle gardens, make a chute of stiff paper which can be tilted to direct the compost where you want it.

- Use a lolly stick or a small spoon fixed to a long stick to make plant holes. A cotton reel fixed to the other end of the stick can be used to tamp the earth down.

- Start the garden off with slow growing plants so that bottle does not get overcrowded too quickly.

Cut flowers

- Cut flowers in the evening. They will contain more nutrients and therefore last longer. Stand them in a bucket up to their necks in water overnight.

- Change the water every other day. Dissolve an aspirin in the water to keep the flowers looking good. Other useful additions are a pinch of salt or a piece of charcoal to keep the water fresh.

- Move cut flowers from a warm room at night.

- Prepare tulips by cutting 2.5 cm/1 in. from the bottom of the stems. Pierce the stem with a pin just below the flower head. This disperses the air bubble trapped in the stem which prevents water reaching the head. Cut off a further 1.25 cm/½ in. from the stem every 3 days.

- To prepare daffodils and narcissi, cut off white parts of the stem and wash away the white sticky sap.

- To prepare roses, remove damaged petals, strip off the thorns and split or crush stems.

- To prepare other woody stemmed flowers, split or crush the bottom of the stem.

- To prepare poppies, singe the bottom of the stem with a candle or gaslighter.

- To revive cut flowers after a few days, snip off the stem ends, stand flowers in boiling water for a few seconds. Then plunge flowers up to their necks in cold water for a few hours.

- To prepare buttonholes, stand the flower in water overnight. In the morning singe the stem end.

- Arrange short stemmed flowers in a shallow dish lined with pebbles (wash them first). Cover with a layer of water and tuck the flowers in among the stones.

Dried flowers

- Flowers for drying should be picked on a hot day so that they contain a minimum amount of moisture. Choose flowers not yet in full bloom.

- Dry the flowers in the microwave if you have one. Instructions are often supplied with the oven.

Window boxes/Patios

- Keep window boxes moist by covering the soil with a thin layer of gravel. This will also prevent the soil splattering the paintwork when it rains.

- Fix window boxes securely at the top of patio walls, then you can grow trailing plants.

- Mount large tubs and pots on a castor-wheeled box (before you put the soil in) for use on the patio. Then you can wheel them about to catch the sun or rearrange the display.

- Patio paving also needs weeding. Gouge out the offending growths with an old table knife. Weed-killer is undesirable on a patio (children, pets, eating al fresco), so dribble boiling water in the cracks to discourage regrowth.

DOMESTIC PETS

General pet tips

- Cats and dogs love sitting around the fire, so provide an adequate fire guard. Secure it to the wall if possible; cats have been known to pull guards over.

- Rubber bands can present a hazard to dogs and cats if they get caught round the animals' paws. They can work their way up the leg hidden by fur and get embedded in the skin. If your pet is limping check the entire leg.

- Clean dog and car hairs from carpets and upholstery with a piece of damp foam rubber.

Summer tips

Take a little extra care of your pets in the summer.

- Be extra vigilant for fleas, which proliferate in hot weather.

- Always provide fresh water daily.

- Make sure there is a shady area for your cat or dog if they are left alone all day. Don't leave cages in 'hot spots'.

- Check regularly for wounds or grazes which can fester quickly in hot weather.

- Check ears, eyes and feet for grass seeds. (These are borne on the wind in the summer, so even urban animals must be checked.) Grass seeds can become embedded in the delicate skin of paws and ears, causing much pain and discomfort.

- Likewise, check for melted tar from roads on paws.

- Never leave your cat or dog in a hot car without ventilation.

- Don't take a dog out for a long walk 'because it's a nice day' if your pet is not used to long walks. Exercise patterns should be built up slowly.

- Don't lock pets in sheds or outhouses in summer

- Remember that conservatories become ovens in the summer. Never leave pet birds in conservatories, they dehydrate very quickly.

- Drape net curtains over pet cages to discourage flies.

- Do not thrust hamsters, guinea pigs or rabbits into unwanted freedom just because it is summer. If they are used to a small hutch and regular, controlled meals, sudden access to the wilderness and unaccustomed wild food sources may make them ill.

Cats

- When acclimatizing a new kitten to your home, cover the fireplace as well as closing the windows. A kitten may make a panicky dash for freedom up the chimney.

- Sexing kittens is not easy. Many a Tom has turned out a Thomasina. A simple check is the space between the anus and the genital area. If you can lay your index finger across the space, the cat is male.

127

- Keeping cats and fleas apart is a never ending task. Here are a few tips:

  — Check with your vet first for the most suitable flea spray.

  — Use newspapers for bedding. Fleas thrive in bedding, so burn it every day and provide a fresh supply. This is especially important in the case of nursing cat mothers and will minimise the fleas passed on to the kittens.

  — To de-flea a cat with flea spray at no damage to yourself, first put the cat in its carrying basket, preferably one with a grid opening. Spray through the basket onto the cat. It will automatically close its eyes and its fur will stand on end in outrage. This helps the spray get to the fleas. When the spraying is over, leave the cat in the basket until it has relaxed once more.

  — Once cats have been de-flead, keep them that way by grooming daily, even if they are short haired breeds.

- Groom your cat for 10 minutes daily if possible, using a smooth-toothed metal comb or a plastic styling comb with widely spaced rows of teeth. (Mark the comb clearly so it is not used by the rest of the family.) Finish the grooming session with firm hand stroking. Daily grooming will discourage fleas.

- If your cat claws and gnaws at the furniture, provide it with a scratching post. They can be bought at pet shops, or make your own by gluing an old piece of carpet or sisal matting on a plank or round a cylinder of wood. The post will be made more attractive to your cat if it is impregnated with catmint.

- Commercial spray is available for spraying furniture to discourage clawing. (Test on a hidden area first.) The smell is undetectable to humans. Do not treat duvets and bedding directly. Treat an old sheet first, allow it to dry then spread over the bed. The sheet may be used to protect the bed when not in use. Eventually the cat will be discouraged.

- To discourage cats soiling in unsuitable places, do *not* rub your cat's nose in it. In cat terms, that means 'this is the place to use'. Try placing the food bowl in the area, as cats never defecate or urinate near their feeding places.

- If you use commercial deterrents to discourage unwanted defecation, go for solutions, pellets or powders rather than aerosols, as they last longer.

- Provide your cat with an acceptable lavatory area or dirt tray and keep it clean. Cats usually go elsewhere if their usual haunt is too disgusting for use.

Dogs

- Do not overbath dogs. It is not necessary unless they are very muddy or dirty. Make your own dog shampoo from 1 part TCP, 2 parts Stergene and 3 parts water.

- You can use the suction tool of your vacuum cleaner to groom your dog (some cleaners have a special attachment). However, do not use the vacuum cleaner when the dog is moulting.

- A lonely puppy can be consoled with a ticking clock, wrapped securely in an old towel, in its basket.

- An old wooden playpen is very useful for young puppies. You can put them in it with their toys if you need to leave them alone for a short while.

- Remember that puppies are just as vulnerable as young children, so keep all small and/or sharp objects (pins, buttons etc.) out of their reach.

- Keep live flex out of young puppies' way; they are very keen on gnawing through it.

- Train your children always to wash their hands after playing with their dog. The parasitic worm *Toxocara Canis*, which some dogs may harbour, can cause blindness.

Fish

- Never keep fish in a goldfish bowl. There is no shelter and, more importantly, insufficient surface area to provide adequate oxygen.

- Only feed fish the amount they can eat in five minutes.

- Do not keep your aquarium in a place where it can be knocked. Vibrations are bad for fish.

- Do not leave an aquarium by a window where direct light can stream in.

- When introducing new fish to your tank, float them in their polythene bags for 15 minutes or so until the water temperatures are equalised. Then open the plastic bags to let the fish out.

- Do not touch fish with dry hands. This will damage the layer of mucus on the fishes skin. Scoop fish out when cleaning the tank with a small net.

Parrots

- Remember that parrots will pine, and are *not* suitable pets if no-one is at home all day.

- Always wear thick rubber gloves when dealing with your parrot.

- Parrots need lots of room; if you cannot afford a suitable sized cage, consider having one custom built by a welding shop.

- Always keep parrot cages out of draughts and direct sunlight.

- Parrot plumage needs to be 'misted' daily, otherwise the feathers get 'pipey' and stiff and moult is impeded. Spray parrots with tepid water in a plant mister. Do this first thing in the morning, so that the parrot has all day to dry off.

Small birds

- To catch escaped birds safely, first note where the bird is roosting; then turn off the light (or pull all curtains and make room as dark as possible). You should then be able to approach the bird quietly.

- Before you allow small birds out of their cage, shut the windows and doors and pull net curtains so that birds cannot hurt themselves blundering against the glass.

- At night, do not switch the lights off and cover the bird cage immediately. Allow the bird to settle down to roost in natural dusk, otherwise it may not be able to find its favourite perch.

- To encourage your canary or other songbird to sing, record his song and play it back to him. Male birds sing not to mate, but to stake out territory and see off rivals. Hearing a male bird singing will, therefore stimulate more birdsong.

- Do not feed your bird with wild grasses, as you cannot be sure whether they have been treated with chemical pesticides or polluted by diesel fumes.

Small rodents

- Do not put hamsters, rats, mice or gerbils on a table or high surface and leave them unattended. Unlike cats they fall heavily and do not land on their feet.

- Hamsters hibernate in the wild and so in cold temperatures may go comatose, apparently dead. Do *not* try to heat them up. Provide plenty of bedding and leave them alone. When they wake (which may be weeks later) provide warm bread and milk.

- A jamjar on its side makes a good lavatory for a hamster. Leave it in the customary 'dirty corner' of the cage.

- A glass 'moat-style' lemon squeezer makes an excellent spill-proof drinking bowl for small rodents (and birds).

8

Security guards

There are all kinds of precautions to take to protect your property. They need not involve much expenditure, just some application of common sense. Remember that good neighbours are probably your best defence against burglary.

GENERAL SECURITY TIPS

- Do not leave portable valuables (stereos, cameras, videos etc.) in full view of passers-by.

- Fit net curtains or blinds on all ground floor windows.

- Mark small items with your postcode followed by your house number with a pen that produces writing that shows up under UV light. They are inexpensive and widely available. Scratch the code on non-absorbent surfaces first, as the pens tend to slide off.

- Have bike frames stamped with your code at your cycle shop.

- Note down the serial numbers on all electrical and photographic equipment and keep the list separate from the equipment.

- Photograph antiques and jewellery. Write details and descriptions on the back of the photographs.

- A baby alarm can be a useful burglar detector. Leave it switched on downstairs while you sleep upstairs. Untoward noises will be broadcast to you.

- Lock doors and windows you cannot see – even if

you are in the house. Burglars can easily slip in through the back door while you are busy at the front or top of the house.

- Lock away ladders and tools which could be used by burglars to break in. Make sure the lock on your tool-shed is as effective as that on your house doors. A padlocked bolt is best.

- If you cannot put ladders away, chain and padlock them to a wall with secure brackets.

- Never leave keys in locks; they are easy to steal and/ or copy. Keep them hidden in a safe place, but make sure all the household know where they are in case in emergency.

- Investigate the various timer/light sensitive systems that are designed to baffle burglars. These can be especially useful if you follow a regular routine. Otherwise, make sure gloomy areas (porch, recessed doors) are well lit.

- If you live in a high risk area, contact the Crime Prevention officer at your local police station. She/he will visit your home and advise you on security aspects. You may consider the pros and cons of a Neighbourhood Watch Scheme.

- If your garage is integral, make sure it is securely locked.

- Check your insurance policy; many insurance companies offer special discounts if you undertake certain security measures.

- If you are considering installing burglar alarms, get three estimates first and ensure you know what after service is included.

- Remember that you can be liable for prosecution as a noise nuisance if your burglar alarm regularly disturbs the neighbours.

- Don't forget to explain how the burglar alarm works to visitors, who may set it off while looking for a nocturnal mug of cocoa.

- Make friends with your neighbours. It is recognised by the police that watchful neighbours are the best burglar deterrent.

Holiday security

- Cancel milk and papers in person. Notes can get into the wrong hands.

- Don't leave a car loaded up with luggage outside your house for longer than necessary.

- Ask a friend or neighbour to check the post, move the curtains/blinds, flush the lavatory and/or run the taps to wet the drains to show potential burglars that the house is occupied.

- Do *not* put your home address on luggage labels. Use your work address or flight number.

- If you leave your car in a long stay car park while away, make sure you do not leave anything with your address in it.

- Never leave messages on your answerphone that tells the caller the dates you will be away. In general, it is not advisable to leave any message that gives the times of your absence from home.

Doors

- Maintain doors and frames in good order. Weak or buckled frames make it easy to remove or kick in the door.

- Make sure that the letterbox does not give access to door bolts. Fit a cage over the letterbox if you are not certain.

- Fit bars or a steel sheet over weak wooden panels.

- Fit only laminated glass indoors (see WINDOWS). Look for BS 6206.

- Check the hinges. Fit outward opening doors with hidden hinge bolts, as outside hinge bolts can easily be knocked out and the door removed entirely.

- If bolts are reachable by smashing a window, make sure they are lockable bolts.

- Fit exit doors with mortice deadlocks. (You neet not disturb existing rim locks to do this.)

- NEVER lock internal doors that you use for a fire escape route.

- Sliding patio doors are child's play to lift out of their runners. Fit deadlocks to the hook bolt. If the doors have claw bolts, fit suitable bolts to the top and bottom of the doors (mortice locks on wooden doors, surface mounted lockable bolts on metal framed doors).

Windows

- Take special care to protect windows on the ground floor or near a flat roof.

- If you have a fixed window (which doesn't open), fit screens to the window frame to secure it to the surround (otherwise it can be lifted out wholesale).

- Fit appropriate window locks (ie make sure they are for sash, casement etc.)

- Double glazed windows should be fitted with locks after consulting the manufacturer, as the wrong lock can reduce the thermal barrier's efficiency.

- If you fit metal grilles or shutters, make sure you have at least two alternative fire escape routes, and that the entire household knows about them.

- Avoid louvre windows, especially in secluded parts of the house. They are easy to dismantle from outside and difficult to defend. Consider replacing them.

- Large windows can be fitted with laminated glass (glass sandwiching plastic layer). Contact Glass & Glazing Federation (see Addresses) for suppliers. The BS number to look for is BS 6206.

- Don't depend on single central lock in vertical sashes. Fit supplementary locks which lock sashes together, or locking stops.

9

Emergency action

The First Aid Box

- Keep your first aid box in the kitchen, where it will be most useful. Avoid ready-made ones: they rarely suit the minor accident requirements of any home. You know what you use most, but here are a few suggestions. Keep them in a secure waterproof container (an old biscuit tin, thoroughly cleaned out).

  — Strip sticking plaster in 2 widths (fabric *and* waterproof).

  — Packets of fingertip and knuckle plasters. Plasters of assorted sizes.

  — Roll of microtape (sticks directly onto wounds or holds dressing on).

  — Crepe bandage.

  — Sterile triangular bandage.

  — Tweezers.

  — Small scissors.

  — Safety pins.

  — Antiseptic wipes.

  — Feverscan type thermometer.

  — Cotton wool buds.

  — Sterile gauze dressings.

  — Children's paracetomol (if you have children).

  — Adult's aspirin or paracetomol.

- Antiseptic spray (for grazes).

- Small bottle of antiseptic disinfectant (TCP, Dettol, Savlon).

- Eyebath and Optrex or similar.

- Aloe vera gel (for minor burns, if skin is unbroken, and sunburn).

- Petroleum jelly.

- Surgical spirit (small bottle).

- Stick the telephone numbers of your doctor, the hospital and the pharmacist on the lid of the first aid box. Cover with clear adhesive tape so they cannot be worn away. Update as necessary. This will help baby-sitters, relations etc. if there is an accident while you are away.

  NB Make sure they can get in touch with you too.

  It is a good idea to keep a small First Aid book in with your first aid kit; even better, make time to follow a first aid course. The emergency situations covered below are the kind that might happen in any home, and it is only sensible to be prepared for them. The Red Cross run local first aid classes and information about them and other short courses, such as Heart Guard, are easily obtained from your doctor's surgery or childcare clinic.

Hypothermia

This most often effects babies and the elderly.

- How to recognise hypothermia:

  - Skin cold to the touch and pale or bluish in colour (although babies may appear misleadingly rosy)

— Victim is confused, drowsy, collapsed or uncon-scious

— No shivering

— Slow, weak or undetectable pulse and slow, shal-low breathing

- What to do:

  — Get medical assistance at once

  — Raise the room temperature as quickly as poss-ible

  — Place the person between blankets. Cover babies lightly, which will warm them up. Do not wrap them in blankets which will impede freedom of movement

  — If they are conscious give warm (NOT hot) sweetened drinks (tea, cocoa)

- What not to do:

  — DON'T put them in front of a fire

  — DON'T apply hot water bottles or electric blank-ets directly to the body

  — DON'T give alcohol of any kind

  — DON'T rub any part of the body

  — DON'T leave them alone

- If your household contains babies or elderly people, prevent hypothermia by keeping the living room temperatures above 21°C/70°F; bedroom tempera-tures should not sink below 12°C/54°F for adults and 16°C/61°F for babies.

Choking

Prompt action is vital.

- For babies:
  Small babies may be held upside down and given three or four slaps between the shoulderblades to dislodge any obstructive object. Alternatively, sit the baby on your lap facing away from you. Hold the tips of two fingers of each hand just above the navel and press firmly but gently upwards. If the baby is unconscious, lay him or her face up on your knees. With the two fingers of each hand placed just above the navel, press firmly and gently upwards.

- For children:
  Lay older children face downwards across your knee and administer the back slaps as above. If that does not produce results, try the abdominal thrust described below.

- For adults:
  Use the abdominal thrust (Heimlich Manoeuvre). Stand behind the victim and put your arms round their waist. Make a fist with one hand and place it, thumb side in, between the navel and the ribcage. Cover it with your other hand then make three or four quick strong pulls, diagonally upwards towards you. This compresses the lungs, forcing air from them which will expel the obstruction. If the victim is unconscious, lay them down on their back, kneel astride their hips and place one hand just above the navel. Push on it with your other hand, thrusting downwards towards the victims head. In both cases, remove anything which comes up from the windpipe into the mouth immediately. Unconscious victims may need artificial respiration (see below).

141

- Self help:
  You can administer the abdominal thrust to yourself;
  alternatively, you can use the back of a chair or a
  table edge. Lean over the edge, supported by your
  hand. Thrust inwards and upwards over the navel
  three or four times.

Poisoning by household chemicals or drugs

- Call an ambulance at once.

- If the victim is conscious, or old enough to talk, ask
  what they have taken.

- Encourage vomiting by giving salt water mixture
  (30 ml/2 tbsp salt to 600 ml/1 pt water) or tickling the
  back of the throat UNLESS YOU KNOW OR BE-
  LIEVE THE POISON TO BE CORROSIVE (acid,
  alkali, petrol, fuel oil, cleaning fluid).

- If strong acid or alkali has been drunk, give lots of
  water to dilute it. If the poison was household
  bleach, follow up the water with milk. Do not induce
  vomiting.

- If petrol or cleaning fluid has been drunk, do not
  induce vomiting as this may cause more damage.

- Keep any vomit, and the bottle or package of the
  poison to take or send to the hospital with the victim.
  Note down the following information:

  — name of poison

  — when it was swallowed

  — when the victim was found

  — whether they were conscious or not.

  This will help medical staff take the correct action.

Burns

- If someone is still covered in flames, roll them in a blanket or coat to extinguish them. Then soak them in water immediately. Do not try to take off charred clothing. It is sterile, and removing it will cause more pain.

- Scalds and burns caused by chemicals should also be soaked in cold water; in this case remove the clothing as soon as possible. Get medical help immediately. Cover damaged skin with dry sterile dressing. DO NOT USE creams or ointments.

- If the burns are extensive and the victim is conscious, lay them on their back with their feet raised. Give them water to sip to replace lost fluid.

- Deep burns caused by electrical equipment and burns larger than 1.25 cm/½ in. square (about the size of a postage stamp) must be seen by a doctor as the damage may be greater than it appears on the surface.

Electric Shock

DO NOT TOUCH THE VICTIM until you have switched off the current and pulled the plug from the socket. Stand on some insulating material (newspaper will do), separate the victim from the appliance with a broom handle or wooden chair (make certain it is dry).

If possible send someone to call for medical help while you try to revive the victim. You may need to use heart massage and artificial respiration (see below). If the victim is conscious, or when they recover, treat them for shock by laying them on their backs with their feet raised and covering them lightly to keep warm. Check for burns: electrical burns are deeper than their surface size indicates.

Heart massage

Kneel at victims left shoulder. Place one hand on the other over the heart so that your fingers touch the bottom of the breastbone. Press firmly and evenly over the heart area, one press a second. Flex your arms as you lean forward. Do not press the chest down more than 5 cm/2 in., less for children. Keep going until the heart starts again. For babies, you can use two fingers rather than your whole hand.

Artificial respiration

The most effective kind is mouth to mouth or mouth to nose, either of which can be used if there is no damage to the face. With babies and young children, it is easier to cover both nose and mouth with your mouth.

Lay the victim on their back. Clear the mouth of foreign objects and remove false teeth if necessary. Lift the neck, tilt the head backwards and pinch the nose. Take a deep breath and cover the victim's mouth or nose with your mouth. Blow into their lungs, then turn your head aside so you can check that their chest falls. (If it doesn't check for blockages in the airway.) You should inflate the lungs once every five seconds.

INDEX